I0820127

Praise for

THE EXTRA MILE

"I REMEMBER WHEN Evan told me he was planning a bike tour in South America. I didn't really know what to think. I've always admired his enthusiasm and commitment to the causes he champions. So, I followed him closely during the days the Ciclo Vida tour was taking place while fervently praying that the Lord would send additional angels to protect him and the rest of the participants. However, reading Evan's firsthand account of everything that took place was not only inspiring, it was thrilling! He lets us follow the group on this adventure that includes flat tires, crashes, hospital visits, and frustrating police interruptions.

We get to experience every miraculous high and soul-crushing low they went through during those days. Sometimes, I laughed out loud. Other times, I felt a knot in my throat as I relived this amazing journey birthed in the mind of a man who cares: cares about people, cares about ministry, cares about his calling, cares about the needy, cares about God. I love crazy ideas and Ciclo Vida certainly fits the category. You're going to love this book!"

—MARCOS WITT, *Latin Grammy Award-winner, Dove Award-winner, and author*

"*THE EXTRA MILE* challenges readers to live boldly for Jesus. This book is a wake-up call to cease living the Christian life apathetically and start loving people the way Christ did—with sacrifice, love, and purpose."

—TASHA LAYTON, *Billboard's Top 5 Female Christian Artist of 2020 and author of* Look What You've Done *and* Boundless

"THE FIRST TIME Evan Craft described his epic bike ride to me, I was captivated. So many of us get up on a stage to lead worship, but Evan was adding an extra layer to his worship of God— he was completing the integrity of the songs he was singing. You have to think that God loves that kind of offering. The singing is relatively easy—the proof is always in the living. I know as you read this book, just like me, you're going to find his journey such a compelling one."

—MATT REDMAN, *Grammy Award-winner, Dove Award-winner, and author*

"EVAN'S HEART comes through in this book, and it's a humble heart. Grateful to hear a story that desires God's fame above our own!"

—Jimmy Needham, *critically acclaimed singer-songwriter, speaker, and forthcoming children's book author*

"THERE ARE TWO ways to look at life: One is to wait for the miracle of God, and the other is to see each day as a miracle from God. Evan encourages us to choose to see God's wonders in *The Extra Mile*."

—Juan de Montreal, *Christian artist, popular content creator, and comedian*

THE EXTRA MILE

An Extraordinary Cycling Journey to Find Faith and Purpose

EVAN CRAFT

with Craig Borlase

K-LOVE BOOKS

THE EXTRA MILE:
An Extraordinary Cycling Journey to Find Faith and Purpose

Published by K-LOVE Books, a partner of Forefront Books, Nashville, Tennessee.

Distributed by Simon & Schuster.

Library of Congress Control Number: 2025907999

Print ISBN: 978-1-63763-391-5
E-book ISBN: 978-1-63763-392-2

Cover Design by Derek Thornton, Notch Design
Interior Design by Mary Susan Oleson, Blu Design Concepts

Printed in the United States of America

25 26 27 28 29 30 LSC 10 9 8 7 6 5 4 3 2 1

For Rachel, the love of my life
and my best friend.
For Sofia and our future babies.
I love you with my whole heart
and I promise to find safer hobbies
than cycling across South America.

Contents

Every Ride Starts Somewhere

(An Introduction)

August 17, 2017. Bogotá, Colombia.

THERE I WAS, on a stage in front of eighty thousand people, halfway through my song "Comfort Zone." I was looking out. I couldn't really see the edges of the crowd or the individuals within it. When the numbers are that big, the faces and arms just blur into one another, as impersonal as a forest bleeding into the horizon. And the weird thing was, even though I'd never played in front of so many people before in my life, it didn't feel at all like I thought it would. It didn't feel like a pinnacle, and it didn't feel like I'd finally made it. I was onstage with my band, which was made up of my best friends, and I was singing the song that I had written in my bedroom years ago. Tears were streaming down my face as I poured out my heart to God and listened to the room fill with the melody I'd just plucked from the air, but in that moment, in that place, the whole thing just felt…

…empty.

The day after the biggest concert of my life, the emptiness had grown. I woke up feeling down. Not the what-goes-up-must-come-down kind of down. This was no adrenaline hangover. Truth is, I hadn't felt much excitement at any point when I was onstage the previous night. My heart wasn't in it like it usually was.

That down feeling stayed with me at breakfast and all through the morning. It was a travel day, so my memories are a mush of sitting with my elbows tucked in as we squeezed into the back of a car for the ride to the airport, waiting for hours to check in and board, then more sitting with my elbows tucked in as we flew to wherever we were playing next. There had been a hundred days like it in the year before that gig, but this one was different. This was the day when I came face-to-face with one of the most uncomfortable truths about myself that I'd ever had to admit:

> *I'm achieving everything that I've ever wanted to accomplish, and it's not nearly enough.*

It wasn't a nice thought. It didn't travel solo either. Soon I was wondering all kinds of things.

> *What if this is as good as it gets?*

> *What if this is the point where my life starts to plateau?*

> *Do I just keep on doing the same thing for the next forty years?*

> *Can I really call what I'm doing "ministry" if I'm just grinding it out, trying to milk it for as long as I can?*

By the time the day was nearly over, I wasn't just feeling down; I was starting to unravel.

* * *

I hope that you're blessed to have a best friend. Maybe it's your spouse, your sibling, your mom or your dad, or someone who once upon a time started out as a stranger to you but who has gone on to become as essential and familiar as the very shoes on your feet. Whoever it is, I hope you've got someone who knows you, who loves you, and whose wisdom and insight you welcome in your life. I hope you've got the kind of person you can call up when life gets all messed up, the kind you can tell the whole unfiltered story to, and you don't need to brace for impact when they give you their response.

Somewhere between Bogotá and California, the next day, I called mine.

"Evan?"

"Yeah, Paul. I really need to talk."

"Okay. I'm listening." Like the very best of best friends, Paul always knows when to say nothing more than the essential.

"We just had the greatest night ever and..." Funny, after such a long day with so many thoughts tangled up within me, I was struggling to find the words. "It was the thing I've been chasing. And now that I've got it, I'm wondering what the point of it all is. I mean, I get paid every night; they treat me like a king. It's easy, and it scares me. What sacrifices am I making to do this? What's noble about any of it if I'm not really helping anyone?"

Paul and I go way back. We'd become friends after we both graduated high school—a couple of eighteen-year-old Jesus Freaks who talked long and often about using our whole lives to serve God. While I'd gone on to do my thing involving music and social media and traveling all over South America, he'd chosen a different path—a quieter one, with not many people watching. He'd not made many plans, but instead tried to keep himself open to whatever God might be leading him into at any given moment. It had taken him on some interesting adventures. Paul's faith was deeper in ways that mine was not, and he had grown within him a deep sense of purpose.

"I don't have what you have," he said when I was done talking. "I don't have that kind of influence. That's why I did the ride."

The ride.

Paul's ride was a thing of legend. A year earlier he'd ridden his bike all the way from Seattle to New York City to raise money for a charity that drills water wells for communities that needed them. Paul is built like a linebacker and walks like a wrestler, and his heart and his faith are 100 percent zeroed in on Jesus, so the ride was a perfect fit for him. I'd been outwardly supportive at the time, but inside I'd kind of winced at the thought of it. There was no way I'd have signed up for something so long and so slow with its return. After all, why spend more than fifty days going through all that pain when I could raise just as much money doing a one-night concert?

Once I'd gotten over myself and actually listened to Paul, I noticed that the ride had changed him. His faith had always been strong: Between the two of us, Paul has always been constant, faithful, and hard-working while I'm more of a roller coaster—the kind of guy whose faith runs deep but whose emotions can also run hot. After the ride there was something else about Paul, like it wasn't just his lungs and his muscles that had been improved as he cycled from west to east; his whole faith was stronger. I'd listened to him talk about the way he wanted to serve God with the rest of his life, and how the ride had given him a clearer sense of purpose. His vision was clearer and his appetite stronger than I'd ever known it.

So on the phone now, as soon as Paul said those two words, something shifted in me. I knew then that I wanted more of that sense of purpose that Paul had. The noise of the airport faded, and the down and empty feelings eased just a little. "The ride" didn't sound so much like foolishness to me. It sounded like it might be able to leave me feeling…

…alive.

This book is about what happened next. It's about the weeks I spent cycling from the Pacific coast of Chile to the Atlantic coast of Argentina, with Paul and others at my side. It's about setting off in pursuit of something meaningful and finding something so much greater than I could have ever dreamed of along the way. It's about purpose and passion and discovering that the best thing I've ever done in life doesn't involve music or stages or seas of faces so vast that it's impossible to tell where it all ends.

But this book is also about more than that, more than just what happened to Paul and me and our friends that summer. Why? Because I think that a lot of us feel trapped like I did by the world we're striving for. We feel disappointed or let down. Too many of us feel as if we're lacking purpose. And from talking to friends, I know there are way too many of us who feel like we're locked in some kind of comfort zone, that somehow this life that we're being told to curate is just too easy and too empty.

My hope is that this book helps. My prayer is that for some of you it becomes the *Tetris* piece that completes the line, the nudge in the right direction that helps fulfill your calling. And what I really want is for all of us to go beyond our own notions of success and our own limits of service. I want us to discover that there, in The Extra Mile, God's ready and waiting.

There, I've said it: *The Extra Mile.*

It's really just another name for the Great Commission, the job description that you, me, Paul, and generations of Christians throughout history have been given. The Extra Mile means going to the places where God leads us, serving the people He places along our path, and living in ways that leave people hungry to know more of God's love for them. The Extra Mile isn't the most comfortable place for us to be, and that's just fine. It's only when we're out of our depth that we learn to swim, and oftentimes it's only when we exit our comfort zones and get rid of our toys and props that we finally learn to trust God.

So if you take nothing else from these pages other than this, then please, read this twice:

Here's to getting out of our depth.

Here's to putting ourselves in places where failure seems likely but faith feels strong enough to drown out the doubts.

Here's to having nothing to lose and putting everything on God. Here's to knowing that we look like fools, but not caring at all.

Here's to doing it all, not for the approval of the crowd but for the audience of One.

Here's to going The Extra Mile.

Are you ready?

Chapter One

"Watch Out, Latin America, Evan Craft Is Coming!"

(And Other Naive Things I Used to Believe)

5:28 a.m. Tuesday, May 10, 2005.

"Evan? Lindy? Cameron? You ready to begin?"

It's early. None of us say much. But we're there. We're ready.

This is one of our family rituals. Dad wakes us up early so that we can study the Bible before school. He doesn't have to do it. He could choose to sleep in instead, but Dad isn't that kind of guy. He sees this as his chance to lay strong foundations in his kids' lives.

Having made some big mistakes already in his life, he doesn't like wasting opportunities.

We talk a lot about character in these early morning sessions. A lot of the time he reminds us about some of the mistakes he's made, and he encourages us to do all we can to avoid them.

But this morning is different. There's no story from his past or example from his present. There's just a verse: Zechariah 4:10. That and a glint in my dad's eye as he looks at me.

"Do not despise the day of small beginnings, Evan. Can't think of a better verse for today."

An hour later, just before six thirty, I'm standing in the corridor outside an empty classroom, waiting. And listening. And praying too. Praying for the people to show up. Praying for the Spirit of God to be present. Praying for nothing less than the fires of revival to fall upon Thousand Oaks High School. Right now, at 6:28 a.m.

Even though it's nearly summer, the air is cold this deep inside the school. It's quiet too, and it feels like I'm the only person on campus. But I'm not deterred. I may be a fourteen-year-old freshman whose skinny little legs and arms are dwarfed by my baggy cargo pants and DC Talk T-shirt, but I'm a believer. I'm a five-foot-nothing Jesus Freak who's on the football team but doesn't party. I'm a third-string receiver who feels just fine about coming off a little weird because I know deep down that genuine miracles are going to happen in this school.

I hear footsteps and glance up to see my friend—a fellow Jesus Freak named Spencer. When I first thought about how cool it would be to invite the whole football team to an early morning youth-group-slash-Bible-study, Spencer was the first one I talked to.

We pray for a minute or two, then go back to staring at the corridor, our ears primed for the sound of incoming football players ready to learn about God.

"Nervous?" he asks.

"Excited." This is the first week we've ever met. There are close to one hundred guys on the team, and Spencer and I have invited every one of them. In all the conversations Spencer and I have had about the

Bible study, we've never really talked about how many members of the team each of us think will show up. We trust God, but we're realists too. Six thirty on a Tuesday morning isn't exactly the ideal time.

The corridor echoes with the sound of a door opening. Then there are footsteps—the telltale squeak of sneakers on the freshly polished floors. Spencer and I look up, ready for the moment they round the corner and come into view. Ready to count the numbers.

"Oh," I say when I see them.

"Yeah," says Spencer.

"That's *a lot* of people."

Our hunch that God was inviting us to partner with Him in a glorious adventure turned out to be right. The Tuesday morning meeting ran for six months throughout my freshman year, and at times we had as many as ninety people show up. We didn't see a whole lot of what I would have then called *genuine miracles*. Nobody had a limb regrown and no tumors fell to the floor midway through a prayer session. But given that the meeting was made up of healthy athletes, there weren't so many of those opportunities in the first place. And it didn't deter either Spencer or me. We were just happy to be serving God and discovering that there's no minimum age requirement for ministry.

The meeting wasn't my only opportunity for spiritual action. I was a pastor's kid and had always spent a lot of time at my dad's church, Northbound. I loved every part of it, from seeing my dad preach and noticing the way the whole room fell silent, to watching the singers and guitar players lose themselves in the music. When I was thirteen I started to learn the guitar, hoping that I would one day lead worship myself. Those times at church were mesmerizing, just like some of my earliest memories of the time when they introduced sign language interpreters. I'd sit and stare like I was at a magic show, captivated by the sight of people communicating with others in a way that I could not.

There were good times in church, but there were complications too. There were a lot of Spanish speakers in the neighborhood, and the way that some white folks who went to church talked negatively about Latinos bothered me. It didn't make any sense to me that a Christian could read Jesus' command to love your neighbor as yourself and then talk disparagingly about the very people living in the same zip code. I didn't want to be like that at all and made up my mind from a young age that if I was serious about sharing my faith, I was going to have to become fluent in Spanish. So in middle school I began taking Spanish, which I continued throughout high school—spending hours at home watching telenovelas, listening to Spanish talk radio, reading all of *Las Crónicas de Narnia*. I was constantly pushing myself to improve. But for me, it wasn't really about grades or the academic affirmation.

By the time I was ready to graduate high school, I had three clear passions in my life: music, ministry, and mission. I wanted to put them together, and so the logical conclusion was for me to become a Spanish worship artist. It didn't matter to me that I was a regular white kid from the suburbs of Ventura County, or that my family were Jewish on one side and German on the other. I wanted to do whatever I could to share the gospel with the very people whom

God had placed on my heart, so the math was simple.

Music + Ministry + Mission =
Spanish worship artist

Sometimes that's just how it goes. When you know God has placed something within you and it's burning hot, the solution is obvious. But then you share your passion with other people and their reactions are different. To them it seems unconventional. Weird. Risky. Maybe they'll even come out and tell you to your face that the whole thing is just foolish. But you know the truth. You know that the math doesn't lie.

When you start to look to God for your sense of purpose and passion, you can expect to see your life differently than others. When you decide you really do want to be a Jesus Freak, you should expect to find yourself on a different path than other people.

You shouldn't be surprised at all.

"God chose what is foolish in the world to shame the wise; God chose what is weak in the world to shame the strong" (1 Corinthians 1:27).

* * *

My first move was to start with the songs. I wrote a few, mainly by googling Bible verses in Spanish and then stitching them together around a simple melody. I also translated my favorite English worship songs into Spanish and then put videos of myself singing them on YouTube. It all went well and grew fast, but what I really wanted was to get out of my bedroom and actually travel to Latin America to lead worship there.

That first opportunity came when I was twenty. I found out about a Foursquare church a little way outside Tijuana. I made contact, explained a little about myself, and offered to travel down and lead worship for them. It took a while to get a response, but eventually, in October, I put my Tacoma acoustic guitar on the back seat of my Tacoma pickup truck and headed south for a week.

I had some thoughts as I drove. A clear sense of what I was going to do and how I hoped this whole thing would weave into God's plan for my life.

If I'm honest, they weren't great thoughts, and

it wasn't a great plan.

I was arrogant. I figured that since I was coming down from a big church that filled hundreds of seats each week, I was going to teach this little congregation on the outskirts of Tijuana what it really meant to lead worship. I was young and this was my first time out on the mission field, but the way I saw it, I might just be the next Billy Graham.

Watch out, Latin America, Evan Craft is coming!

I arrived when the nightly meeting had already started and eased my way into the side.

The meeting was in a tent with a dirt floor. There were a few rows of plastic chairs and construction lights burning in the corner. There was a loud buzz coming out of the PA system, and the drum kit was so beaten up it looked like whoever had last played it had been using claw hammers instead of sticks.

The pastor—a woman named Claudia—was leading people in prayer. They were pleading with God to send revival to their city. I counted maybe twenty young people and twice as many older ladies. Hardly any men my father's age.

I stood and stared and listened to them as they prayed. Some were standing. Others were kneeling on the dirt.

The air was heavy.

I could feel my breath sitting low in my lungs.

The presence of God was as tangible as I'd ever known it.

I could feel myself beginning to be crushed from the inside out as I became convicted of the truth:

How dare you come into My presence like this!

How dare you come down here thinking you're going to take My place and steal My glory!

I felt naked and ashamed, convinced that anyone who looked at me would be able to see the arrogant fraud that I was. But when Pastor Claudia came over and introduced herself, she treated me with nothing but warmth.

"Will you lead us in worship, Evan?"

I nodded, and soon I was fumbling my way through the only three Spanish worship songs I knew well enough to play. And as I did, with my eyes open, I saw the faces even more clearly. They were worshiping with a passion and intensity that I'd never encountered before. My guitar sounded out of tune and my voice was cracking, and there was no doubt in my mind who was leading who that night. They were pouring themselves out to God, and they were gracious enough to let me tag along.

When I'd run out of songs to play, they clapped. But it wasn't for me, and it wasn't at all like the polite clapping that would ripple through the auditorium back home. This was loud. The longer it went on, the louder it became.

Soon people were praying. Like the applause, it couldn't have been more different from what I was familiar with. People were shouting their prayers, their voices tumbling over one another. They were pleading with God to reduce the violence, to stop the killing, to end the devastation caused by drugs, to provide enough food for them to eat and deal with the corruption that was paralyzing their government.

I stood still. Eyes closed. Head bowed.

I had known plenty of Christians I had looked

up to—guys who could preach and have the whole church listening, or worship leaders with voices so powerful and gifts so rich that it was impossible not to marvel. I'd been in plenty of church services that were slick and polished and impeccably put together, but I'd never been a part of anything like this. I'd never been in the presence of Christians who were so dependent on God for things that I took for granted. I'd never been in the company of people whose needs were so basic and whose faith was so strong.

It almost took my legs out from under me. Standing there, listening to the voices explode inside the tent, I realized that my life so far had been utterly different from theirs. I'd never known hunger. Never known danger. Never known poverty. And I'd never once in my life known what it means to be truly desperate for God.

The meeting carried on for another hour or two, with me floating along like a piece of driftwood in the storm. I sang a couple of the songs again, fully aware that I wasn't leading anyone in worship. They were leading me every step of the way.

For the next week I'd spend my days learning

new songs, talking with Pastor Claudia, or taking trips out to explore the neighborhood. It was all new to me, all different and exciting. But it was the evening meetings in the tent that I was most excited about. Those hours were the highlights of my day, my month, my year.

Each night the same people showed up to worship and pray with the same passion that I had seen when I'd first walked into the tent. They didn't get bored or want Pastor Claudia to change things up, because it was obvious that none of them were there to be entertained or distracted. They were there to do business. They were there to plead with God for transformation for their community and offer themselves to be His hands and feet.

When I reached the final moments of my last night, Pastor Claudia came over and thanked me.

"We want to give you this," she said, holding out her hand.

Instinctively, I reached out. I don't know what I was expecting—maybe a booklet or a card of thanks—but as soon as my fingers closed around the envelope, I knew it was cash. I looked inside. Eighty dollars.

After a week of being surprised by the church, this was on a whole other level. I knew how little they had, and eighty dollars was a colossal amount. I just couldn't understand why they would do something like this. I handed it back to Pastor Claudia. "I can't take this."

"You can," she said, giving me a look that told me I had no option other than to take it.

I wanted to tell her that I really didn't deserve it. I wanted to tell her about how arrogant I'd been when I was driving down, and how much of a deep, deep privilege it had been to spend time with her and the church that week. I wanted to tell her that I had already received greater blessings than I could have ever hoped for, and that all this money on top was too much.

But Pastor Claudia wasn't wavering. There was nothing to discuss.

Driving home the next day, spending hours waiting at the border crossing, I was exhausted and had plenty of time to think about the past week. The whole thing was so wild and intense that I was struggling to process it all. I didn't know whether God had metaphorically slapped me in the face or whispered gently in my ear. There had been moments when it had felt like He was doing both at the same time: exposing me to the ugliness of my arrogance as well as inviting me to go further up and further into His love.

As I made my slow journey north, back to my home in the land of wealth and power and privilege, I knew that God was saying this one thing for sure:

Unless you learn to love My people, nothing's going to happen for you here. They're not here for you to build your career on. They're not here for your entertainment. They're not here for you to practice starting a revival with. I want you to learn to love them as I do.

Even though it only lasted a week, that first trip was life-changing. It was like having your map blown out of your hands and over a cliff during the first minutes of an epic hike. I was forced to instantly abandon all my preconceived ideas of where I was going and how I was going to get there, and trust God instead. It all happened so fast, and I sometimes wonder how else God would have knocked out my arrogance had I not decided to drive down to Tijuana feeling like I was the spiritual heir to Billy Graham. Maybe there was another way, but I'm grateful for the fact that it happened right then, when I was just twenty and my life plans were still sitting in wet concrete.

As well as knocking back my ego and realigning my priorities, the whole thing taught me another vital lesson: that even though there might be some glaring errors within us, if we're putting ourselves in the places where God calls us, then we're giving ourselves the best opportunity to stay close to where we need to be. That's why Scripture tells us to keep on "looking to Jesus, the founder and perfecter of our faith" (Hebrews 12:2). He's the One who can take the broken and imperfect and make it whole again. In other words, God doesn't mind us showing up with a mess to deal with or some issues to resolve. He just wants us to show up.

That's why, a few weeks after I arrived home from Mexico, I was driving back down to join Pastor Claudia. Only this time I was planning on staying a whole month.

* * *

Five years later, I was on the phone with Paul telling him that I had just played in front of eighty thousand people in Bogotá and that something about it all didn't feel right. I was a long, long way from Pastor Claudia's tent outside Tijuana.

So many good things had happened in those five years, and I had a lot of reasons to be grateful to God. I had put more covers up on YouTube and seen the numbers fly. I had written more songs and landed a record deal. I had formed a band with a bunch of guys who had gone on to become my best friends, and together we had toured Latin America. I'd met many Christian giants like Pastor Claudia, men and women of God whose faith dwarfed mine. I'd spent time in some of the most beautiful places on earth and immersed myself in some of the most wonderful communities and cultures you could ever hope to experience.

Even so, I was a long, long way from Pastor Claudia's tent. A long, long way from knowing that I was taking risks and putting myself in a place where

I really, truly needed God. A long, long way from being in the kind of excited, nervous state where I had absolutely no idea what God was about to do next.

I hadn't slipped back into my old, arrogant mindset, and it wasn't as if I had forgotten that vital lesson about the importance of loving God's people. But somehow I'd lost the clear sense of having a God-given purpose. Like a flashlight whose batteries are gradually fading, my vision for serving God through music that had once been so clear and so bright had grown dim. The change had been so slow that I hadn't noticed it at first, but by the time I was onstage with all those people spread out before me, the truth was undeniable: I wanted to get back to that place where my faith felt truly alive again.

Chapter Two

Comfort Zones
(and How to Avoid Them)

The concert was the most dramatic wake-up point, but it wasn't the only one. One day, at the end of a five-week tour of Argentina, Bolivia, and Ecuador, I woke up after a nap. I was in a hotel in Ambato, and as I got up from the bed, I was hit by the strongest desire to return home. I missed my pillows. I missed my house in Houston. I missed fresh vegetables. I wanted to be able to close my eyes and transport myself back to my big TV and reliable internet and be able to select clothes from a closet instead of pulling them out of a suitcase. I wanted to go back to the time when I had no responsibilities: no band wages to pay, no tours to organize, no crowds to stand up in front of and have something inspiring or insightful to say.

Don't go back to your comfort zone.

The words were almost audible.

Don't go back to your comfort zone.

In that moment my whining faded into the background. In its place came gratitude. God had taken me on the most amazing adventure, and there was more to come. Sure, I could choose to return to the comfortable life if I wanted, but I knew that I'd be missing out.

There was another time when I was in Paraguay, sitting quietly in a pastor's office before I was about to go out and play at a big worship night. The church was in a town called Encarnación and it was easily the hottest venue I had ever played in. The temperature outside was pushing 100 degrees Fahrenheit and when I'd stood in the back of the hall earlier, I guessed that among the crush of people it must have been even hotter. The AC wasn't working, and I swear I even saw someone faint.

Sitting in the pastor's office, I was not feeling good about it. The heat was bothering me, but that wasn't all. I was having a diva moment, and the prospect of a whole set made up of other people's songs was making me grouchy. It struck me as pathetic to be the kind of artist who entertained Christians with other writers' songs.

I was in the middle of a prayer along the lines of *God, I don't know why You even brought me here* when the pastor walked in.

"Evans?" he said, adding a brand-new *s* to my name. "I'd like you to meet these two people. They drove three hours to be here tonight."

I stood up, wiped the sweat from my hands, and greeted the couple. They were a little older than me, but not by much. The guy spoke first, telling me that they both loved the cover I'd recorded of a song called "Glorious Ruins" by Hillsong Worship.

"Oh," I said. "Thanks."

"It was such a special song for us," said the woman. "Our son had cancer, and it was his favorite song all through treatment. He loved the idea of God making something glorious out of something so painful."

She paused. The dad picked up the story. "When he heard that you were going to be here, playing tonight, he was so excited."

"Great!" I said, feeling a little dumb for being such a diva. "Let's go meet your son."

There was silence. Then a look exchanged between the parents.

"He passed two weeks ago," said the mom. "We'd love for you to play it tonight. We brought sixty people with us. Will you play it?"

I opened my mouth to tell them that of course I'd play it, but hardly any words came out.

Later, drenched with sweat and tears, I stood onstage as the heartbeat drum rhythm started up. My voice cracked as I sang, my hands struggling to play the chords. The band carried us through to the start of the first verse. Then the voices took over—a choir of sixty strong all standing down near the front. By the time we hit the chorus and the melody climbed and soared, they were carrying every single one of us in worship.

I was back in the tent.

It's not about you, Evan. Whatever "artistry" you value, whatever story you're telling about this journey you're on… it's not about you. It's about whether you're willing to be a conduit for God's message and His power and His love.

* * *

We live in a strange world.

As consumers we're weaned on comfort. We're brought up to crave it. To chase it. To fight for it. To spend our time and our money and our best efforts in pursuit of it. The house. The car. The appliances. The subscriptions. The memberships. The 401(k). And when all the comfort that we've amassed gets threatened and we fear that it will be taken away—the bank forecloses on the house, the credit cards are frozen, and the way of life we worked so hard to achieve is no longer possible—it can leave us terrified.

And yet, when we meet God, we discover something wild—something upside-down. We discover that comfort doesn't deliver the way we've been told it will. There's no need to chase it or make it our goal.

Then, when we go a little deeper in our faith,

we discover something incredible. We discover that if we really want to receive the very best that God has to give us—if we really want to be blessed—then having fewer of those comforts is the way to go.

It's all there in Matthew 5, when Jesus delivers His most perfect sermon:

"Blessed are the poor in spirit,
for theirs is the kingdom of heaven.
Blessed are those who mourn,
for they shall be comforted.
Blessed are the meek,
for they shall inherit the earth.
Blessed are those who hunger
and thirst for righteousness,
for they shall be satisfied."
(vv. 3–6)

These words used to confuse me. I didn't like the idea of being poor, sad, meek, or in need of righteousness. It was only when I studied these verses that I understood the truth: Jesus is describing the ideal conditions in which we can draw closer to Him.

It's when we're empty that we realize we're nothing without Him.

It's when we mourn that we understand that God's heart breaks for those who are mourning too.

It's when we put aside our belief in our own strength and become meek that we make more room for God to demonstrate His mighty power in our lives.

It's only when we find ourselves in real need of comfort that we understand how to give it to others.

When I was twenty, I wanted to see justice roll out, to see wrongs put right and lives transformed. My intentions were good, but my assumptions were a little wrong. I assumed that if I was going to see great things happen, I'd need to do great things myself. But time and study and moments like that night when I was in Paraguay worshiping with that grieving family changed my view. I came to understand that our role is to obey. God's the one who causes the walls of Jericho to come crashing down. All we have to do is be obedient and answer His call.

The Sermon on the Mount isn't a rage against comfort or a warning that anyone who's wealthy is going to face trouble. But it *is* a recalibration of what we understand of the way that God works. He doesn't turn His back on those of us who are struggling under the weight of pain, poverty, grief, depression, or any other of a whole load of life situations we spend all kinds of time and effort trying to avoid. God doesn't run away from all that stuff. Instead, He runs toward it. He meets us there. And for those of us whose lives are untouched by grief, pain, poverty, and all the rest, He calls us to get in there and join Him.

So if you're starting this book and are feeling confused by the presence of injustice, poverty, and pain around you, you're probably in a far better place than you might imagine. Jesus is both blessing you and telling you that He will satisfy you. He's bringing you further along, and you're entering The Extra Mile.

* * *

Between the grieving couple in Paraguay, the revelation about my comfort zone in Ecuador, and the epic-concert-that-wasn't-the-pinnacle-I'd-thought-it-would-be in Colombia, I was ready to make a change. I wanted to do something that brought me back to being dependent on God again, something that would bring back that sense of purpose that had gradually faded from my life. Most of all, I wanted to do something that made a tangible, practical, positive impact on lives.

A coast-to-coast charity bike ride like Paul's sounded like the perfect solution.

So I got to work.

I figured that the best way to raise the most money possible would be to play a series of concerts, with a bunch of us riding our bikes to each venue. We could use our standard fee to cover the tour's expenses, find a local charity to support, and use the concerts as an opportunity to fundraise. If we did ten concerts, I figured that we could raise close to $100,000.

Then there was the route to decide. Paul and I talked it through and came up with a bunch of different ideas. We considered going coast to coast in Mexico, north to south in Colombia, and even doing the whole of Panama. But the more we looked, the more I liked the idea of starting in Chile and riding east across Argentina. It was a long route, but it had two clear advantages that I could see. First, the route would take us through Santiago, Mendoza, Córdoba, and Rosario, which were all places where I had good contacts with great churches. Second, once we'd climbed the Andes mountains, it would be flat all the way to the Atlantic Coast.

I was back home in Houston, in the house that I shared with my band. I explained the idea of the ride with them, and they seemed excited too. None of them were cyclists, but that didn't matter. Paul had already warned me how tough it is to ride hundreds of miles over several days, and we'd agreed that the band would drive between gigs, leaving the riding to a core group made up of a handful of experienced, capable cyclists like Paul and our pro cyclist friend, Essence.

And me.

I hadn't ridden a bike since high school, and I didn't even own one. But I was fit from playing a lot of soccer and confident enough in myself to commit. I was also keen to get on and do it, so as soon as we'd agreed on the route, I started talking to churches about the possibility of them hosting concerts the following summer.

"You're sure about this?" asked Paul on one of our many calls about the ride. He was sounding more than a little skeptical.

"Absolutely. Nine months of training starts now."

I'd just bought my first road bike: a mid-priced Specialized with a saddle that was about as wide as the palm of my hand. Even though I had bought the recommended pair of padded shorts, my first few rides around some of Houston's bike paths left me in agony. Having most of my body weight pressing down through my sit bones onto an uncushioned piece of molded plastic was like nothing I'd ever experienced before. For a while, I wondered if Paul was right to be so skeptical.

A month after I got the bike, the saddle pain was finally easing. Somehow I'd gotten used to it and was able to crank out ten miles a few times a week without feeling like my hips were about to tear apart. But while the physical pain was subsiding, some new relational conflict had sprung up in the house.

I'd always gotten on well with my band and considered us to be the best of friends. We had been together for almost four years. We had traveled all over Latin America in that time, seeing everything from Machu Picchu to the expansive Patagonia. When we were not on the road, we all lived together in the house I'd bought in Houston, and it felt like we were living the dream: a tight crew of twenty-somethings with well-worn passports and photo libraries full of great memories.

Even though I was the artist whose name appeared on the publicity, I always thought of us as a band. Back in the early days we'd talked about becoming a regular band—the kind that split all the duties and the risks and the money equally among us. It was a risk that I was happy to take, but the others weren't so keen on the arrangement. They told me that they liked being Evan Craft's backing band and were happy to pick up a daily wage for every concert we did. It was important to me that they felt valued and would want to sign up for the long haul, so we agreed on a rate that was way above average.

Everything had been going well for those first three years, but around the time that Paul and I started to plan the bike ride, things began to change a little. It seemed to me that playing in front of eighty thousand people had affected them as well as me, but in different ways. Some of the guys told me that they wanted more money. I told them that I couldn't afford to pay them $1,000 a night when we were only making $5,000 from a concert. They told me that if we were playing in front of that many people, we ought to be able to charge more. I told them that making more money wasn't my aim.

It wasn't a one-off conversation. It repeated itself from time to time throughout the fall. I knew they were frustrated, and I hated the fact that we were clashing like this, but I had a hunch that it would all work out soon enough. I thought that the ride would be good for us all, and that even if the guys weren't on bikes, they'd be inspired and excited by it. The ride had all the hallmarks of a God-plotted adventure, and I knew it would change their lives. Maybe all of our lives.

I'd just gotten back from a ride one morning when one of the guys told me that he had some news he wanted to share.

"Sure," I said as I fixed myself a sports drink.

"I quit."

We talked, but his mind was made up.

He wasn't the only one either. Over the next few days others told me that they were done as well. One had decided to get married and didn't want to tour anymore; others told me they'd joined other bands.

Within two weeks they'd left. Not just a few of them. All of them. And not just quit the band either: They'd moved out entirely.

Just when I had made up my mind to do something that would put me back on track with God, I'd lost my band and my best friends. I'd always thought that we'd be playing and touring together as a band for the rest of our lives. I'd always assumed we were equally invested in this passion project. I'd always believed that we were united in our desire to say yes to God.

I was wrong.

In that moment, I don't think life had ever looked so bleak.

Chapter Three

An Artist or a Soldier

(It's Tough Being Both)

I pulled my bike out of the trunk, reattached the front wheel, and listened as Paul ran through the plan.

"It's a thirteen-mile loop. Mostly flat, but a climb between miles three and six. If you've been doing ten in Houston, this'll be fine."

We were in Pasadena, in a parking lot by the Rose Bowl. Christmas was over and I'd traveled out to California to spend some time with my dad and take my training to a new level by getting out on the bike with Paul. It was our first ride together, and I was feeling good. At least, I had been feeling good until I'd seen Paul dressed in his Lycra.

The man was a beast.

He'd always been broad and strong, but as he climbed onto his bike and made a few last-minute adjustments to his helmet, he looked like an Olympic sprinter about to compete for gold. His legs were twice as big as mine, and his size dwarfed the bike beneath him. He was five foot eleven and 215 pounds; I was five foot six and 142 pounds. Next to him I looked like a scrawny kid who spent most of his time gaming indoors and who'd just borrowed his older brother's wheels for the weekend.

We set off and for the first few moments it was okay. I was able to keep pace with my best friend.

Then we left the parking lot.

"You good?" asked Paul as we moved out onto the empty pathway.

"Fine."

"Great. Let's get going."

Paul adjusted his gears, increased the power running through his legs, and surged ahead of me like he'd just hitched onto a passing truck. I dug deep and summoned all the strength that I could to keep pace with him. Within minutes my legs were full of lactic acid, my lungs were burning, and my stomach was gripped by waves of nausea.

Paul slowed and by the time we reached the ascent at mile three, he was pedaling beside me, giving a steady stream of encouragement. I was heaving and seeing stars and the guy wasn't even remotely out of breath.

We paused at the top and Paul handed me an energy gel. I sucked the goo into my mouth and chugged a bottle of water.

"I'm thinking…" I said between drinking and gasping for air. "That this was… the biggest mistake I've ever made in my life."

I looked up at Paul. He was smiling.

"Why did I think I could do this?"

More smiles.

"And why have I gone all over Instagram telling people about how we're going to ride one thousand miles over the Andes? I can't even manage thirteen. The guys were right to quit on me."

No more smiles. From either of us.

We started riding again soon after. Downhill

was certainly easier, especially as Paul was still holding back. My lungs had stopped screaming quite so hard and the nausea was fading. My legs still felt like they were on fire, but by tapping into my sorrow about the band, I managed to keep going. The more it hurt physically, the more I silently mourned the end of the band. It was just raw emotion and physical exhaustion. It was all I had.

Over the next few weeks that I was in California, Paul and I rode a lot. And in the same way that my butt got used to my seat, my legs and my lungs slowly adjusted to the stresses and demands of an hour or more on the road with Paul. He helped me graduate from thirteen to twenty and then thirty miles, and even though I'd end up back at my dad's house exhausted and craving nothing more than a bowl of pasta and a long afternoon nap, I was content. I was putting all my anger, frustration, and disappointment into those hours on the bike. It was a deep kind of prayer, but one with hardly any words and a whole lot of sweat.

* * *

I have been blessed to have known some wonderful people throughout these years that I have been making music. Producers, promoters, agents, and more, there has never been a shortage of people who God has used to deliver the right word at the right time. And among them all, one of the people whose words and timing always seems to be the best is Marcos Witt.

The first time I encountered Marcos I was doing some research into what it would take to establish a career in Christian music. I had googled "Christian music Spanish" and there, toward the top of the results, was Marcos Witt—the absolute epitome of a Christian artist recording in Spanish. He was in his forties at the time, but he was already the GOAT. Sixty million albums sold. Six Grammys won. In terms of industry definitions of *success*, if Marcos, Witt hadn't achieved it, it probably wasn't worth bragging about.

I met Marcos in 2014 and he was even more impressive in person than he was on the internet. He was kind, thoughtful, and genuinely interested in a YouTuber like myself, even though he had zero reason to be. We became friends, but it went deeper than that. To me, Marcos was a mentor, a Yoda figure to whom I could always turn to for advice.

I turned to him often.

Like the time when I turned up in Bolivia with the band to find that the church that had invited us hadn't even booked a venue. It was a mad scramble from start to finish, and a couple of hours before we were due to play—when my band was threatening to walk and leave me to do it solo—Marcos was the first person I called and explained the trouble I was in and how frustrated I was getting with everyone.

He laughed. "If I had a dollar for every time I felt that way," he said. "Let me ask you a question, though."

"Okay."

"Are you an artist, or are you a soldier?"

That was it, right there. The single, simple question that hit pause on all my stress. It opened my eyes to see the scene in 360 degrees, to step out from my me-first thinking and remember the truth about why I was there in the first place: I wasn't there to be an artist and build a career. I was there to be a soldier and serve God.

I don't know God's vision for Marcos Witt's life. I don't want to set my goals based on whatever he's achieved. But I do want to emulate his character.

This habit of trying to copy people trips a lot of us up from time to time. We get fixed on a narrative of what our lives should be like. We focus on it so hard that when something happens that interrupts and threatens to derail our plans, we freak out.

The root of this? I'm convinced that a lot of it has to do with comparison. It shouldn't surprise anyone to read that when we spend hours looking at someone else's life—or, to be precise, the carefully curated account of their life that they are choosing to share with the world—our own story pales in comparison.

As Christians, we're no less immune. We can put people on pedestals and confuse worldly success with spiritual blessing. We look at the guys who we think have made it and set our sights on achieving similar success. We do this and we miss one of the most important points of Jesus' life: His offer to people was not primarily to achieve a set of goals. He didn't say "join My team and we'll build an insurgent religion that will grow by millions within the first few centuries." What He said was: "Follow me" (Matthew 4:19).

To the disciples, as well as to others like the rich young ruler, Jesus said, "Follow me." It wasn't a promise of results or some kind of status promotion. It was an invitation to begin a relationship that would transform their lives completely.

He's still saying exactly the same thing today.

To me.

To you.

What's your response? Are you an artist or a soldier?

* * *

Eventually, toward the end of January, I returned to Houston. I had a couple of new roommates, but the house was empty and quiet and lonely without the band. I didn't like it at all.

"Evan?"

"Hey, Marcos."

The call was long overdue, and it took a while to explain about the plans for the ride and everything that had happened with the band. When I was done,

Marcos asked me how I was feeling.

"Frustrated. I don't think I want to be in Houston anymore. Things feel stuck."

"You're like a car in first gear. Over the last few years, it's taken a ton of energy to get yourself moving, investing in the band and all that. You've been Hurricane Evan. But now you need to change. You need to shift gears and focus more on things that will be healthier for you. You need to find a band that you don't have to drag with you."

The conversation gave me plenty to think about. I had been feeling a little sorry for myself since returning to Houston, so there was a part of me that didn't want to have to take on the massive task of going out and recruiting and training a new band. After all, my guys were the ones who had quit on me. It didn't feel right that I should have to go all the way back to the beginning and start over. But the more I thought about Marcos's words, the more I realized that shifting gears didn't mean going back to the way things were. It meant a clean start and a new beginning. An opportunity to do things better this time and avoid some of the mistakes I had made before.

I liked the idea of that a lot.

And I knew exactly where I wanted to do it.

* * *

There was a time when Medellín, Colombia, was known as the City of Eternal Gunfire. Sometime around the time I was in kindergarten, *TIME* magazine declared it the most dangerous city on earth. They had good reason. Medellín was home to Pablo Escobar, the world's most notorious drug lord at the time. Assassinations were common and corruption was rampant. Back then, a guy like me wouldn't have lasted more than a few weeks in Medellín.

Things are different now.

I chose to move to Medellín because of all the places I'd visited over the years, it was the coolest, the most vibrant, and full of entrepreneurs. Perhaps it's because of its troubled past, but the city is simply the most energized and optimistic place you could ever hope to visit. It's full of innovators and artists, full of people who are positive and optimistic. I needed to shift gears, and Medellín was the perfect place to do so.

Even though I'd studied abroad in Spain and spent an average of thirty weeks each year touring, I'd never really lived abroad. Moving to Colombia was a major shift, but it was made easier by the fact that when I told my tour manager, Adrian, about my Medellín plans, he agreed to move from Costa Rica and join me.

Life was almost instantly good. Adrian and I did Airbnbs for a few weeks, then rented an apartment for the next six months. I found a church to attend and devoted my time to living the way Marcos advised. No more Hurricane Evan: As soon as I was in Medellín I put my focus on the right things. Each day was open, and I filled it in the best way possible. I went to the gym; I wrote songs with people; I ate out with new friends and learned right away that in Medellín, I would be eating some of the very best food of my life. My mouth would start watering as soon as I'd ordered a plate of *arepas*—thick corn pancakes filled with *chicharron* (pork belly), beans, rice, eggs, a little ground beef, and some of the biggest, greenest avocados I'd ever seen. It was so good, and I'd sit back from my empty plate, laughing with my new friends, no longer feeling quite as much like the gringo who came in from out of town for a concert before flying off again. I was becoming a member of the community.

The people I met were great. Some had started studios to support young musicians, others had launched community soccer clubs. There were marketers and engineers, creatives and tech innovators. I met a bunch of super-famous bands at the airport, bumped into one of the country's top soccer players in a coffee shop, and ended up flying to Monaco to record a single. So many doors were opening for me because all of these people, from the best known to the least, shared the same positive, optimistic view of life. If someone went to them with an idea or a problem that needed fixing, the default response was to do anything possible to help out. Coming from Houston and all the stress and negativity that was surrounding my band, it was like resurfacing after being underwater for too long.

Medellín is beautiful. It's set at the north end of the Andes, in a deep valley that's dominated by mountains. When you're down in the valley, you don't get to see any sunsets, but the brightly colored houses have a beauty of their own. The place is magical, and with only a few months to go before the bike ride, I was keen to increase my training.

It was good to find out that the city is bike-friendly. Every Sunday and Tuesday they closed roads to allow *ciclovía* (bike lanes), which got me thinking. So far, the bike ride that Paul and I had been planning was only ever referred to as the Bike Ride. Clearly we needed a better name, and Medellín gave me an idea. *Ciclo Vida* (bike life) summed up everything we were about: using the bike ride to raise money and transform lives.

Coming up with a name was easy. Getting my body acclimated to the terrain around the city was not. I heard about a cycling group made up of a mixture of locals and European pros who had chosen Medellín as a training base. I joined them on a ride out to the airport one day—ten miles each way. I knew my legs and lungs were good for the distance, but the incline had me worried.

It was a beast.

The road started climbing steeply almost at the

very start, and it didn't level out until it reached the airport—3,200 feet above the starting point. With Medellín at almost 5,000 feet elevation, that meant the final few miles were at an altitude of 8,000 feet—the level at which high-altitude training typically begins. When you're this high up, there's less oxygen in the air and fatigue kicks in a lot sooner. But there's a benefit to it and a reason why a lot of those European pros came to Medellín for training. At high altitude your body is forced to adapt to the lack of oxygen, so blood vessels become more efficient and you can exert more energy at sustained exposure to high altitudes. It also improves heart function and overall health. Not bad. My assumption was that by doing all my training in Medellín, I'd find the part of *Ciclo Vida* that came after the Andes to be a piece of cake.

Despite my optimism, that first time cycling to the airport in Medellín was anything but easy. It took me one hour and twenty-five minutes to reach the top, and just fifteen minutes to get back down again. It was insane, and I experienced new depths of pain that made what I'd experienced on the Rose Bowl bike ride with Paul pale into insignificance.

But I knew it was doing me good.

I tried to vary things. Sometimes I'd ride with the big guys; other times I'd head out on my own. There was a sixty-mile loop I heard about that went way out of the city and was rumored to have some of the best views in the country. Over a period of weeks, I built up my stamina until I felt confident enough to tackle it. And what a ride it was. It went way out of the city and took me through all kinds of landscapes. I rode beneath mountains and alongside coffee plantations and alpine pastures full of cattle. And every few moments there would be some kind of exotic tropical bird flying overhead. I was a long, long way from home, and I'd spend miles and miles wondering how I'd gotten there.

It wasn't all beautiful views and moments of calm reflection. When I decided to step up my training, I started looking for local short routes where I could work on my speed. I didn't have a car in Medellín, so I was limited to the airport road. The cycling group only met once a week, so I started tackling it solo, which was when I discovered the disadvantage of being a solo cyclist on a busy road. After too many close calls with speeding cars, I asked a couple of cyclists I'd met for advice. Medellín being Medellín, the answer was unusual but inventive: Someone had a friend named Juan Pablo with a motorbike who, for six dollars an hour, was willing to ride behind me and be my offensive tackle, even when I wanted to get out at 5:00 a.m. before the traffic and the summer heat got bad. It worked great. Having Juan Pablo behind me meant that the cars kept their distance and my stress levels dropped.

One day, however, I must have gotten a little too relaxed. I was cycling along one of the city's busiest streets, trying to ease my way past a lot of traffic. My training had been going well and I was feeling strong, especially with Juan Pablo behind me. That meant I was a little too heavy on the speed and way too easy on the concentration. I wasn't scanning ahead and so, out of what felt like nowhere came a chuckhole that was big enough to cause me serious damage. I swerved, lost control, and rode at full speed into a divider that was separating the bus lane from the main traffic. Luckily the thing was made of plastic, not concrete, but it was still way stronger than I was, and I ended up getting thrown off my bike and landed on my side in the road.

I guess I was kind of stunned, because the loudest thought going through my mind was that I hoped my bike was okay.

Then I heard Juan Pablo shouting, screaming, "*¡Para, para!*" and felt his hands hauling me up off the road.

I looked up to see a bus heading straight for where I had landed.

I was shaken up pretty bad for an hour or two, my mind stewing on thoughts about how dangerous it can be to cycle on a busy road.

We planned to have five or six of us riding on *Ciclo Vida*, and a new revelation dawned on me: Even though they would all be better cyclists than me, as the guy who was organizing the whole thing, I would be responsible for their safety. If something went wrong, it would be on me.

I know it's an obvious connection to make, but the way we train our bodies to be fitter, faster, and stronger has clear spiritual lessons for us. We can only improve our muscles when there's something to push against, and the same is true for our faith and trust in God. We might not like it when things are against us—maybe it's adversity of some kind, or there's some unexpected opposition that is blocking our way—but things are hard in life and when we turn to God, we grow.

I don't know who the first person was to say that "God doesn't call the qualified, He qualifies the called," but whoever it was captured a powerful truth. We're a work in progress. We're clay in the Potter's hands. If we want God to use us and shape us and mold us for His purposes, then we're going to have to expect some challenges. People are going to quit on us. Our mistakes are going to cause us trouble. Our egos will take over and we'll end up crashing into a whole bunch of obstacles that are there for our safety.

The Bible is full of this, and one of the examples I like best is Joseph. After being tricked, betrayed, and sold into slavery while he was still a (kind of arrogant) kid, Joseph then spent thirteen years in prison. Toward the end of his story, as he addressed the brothers who had sold him in the first place, his perspective was clear:

> "As for you, you meant evil against me, but God meant it for good, to bring it about that many people should be kept alive, as they are today. So do not fear; I will provide for you and your little ones." Thus he comforted them and spoke kindly to them. (Genesis 50:20–21)

Joseph's story makes it clear that bad things happen. It's not that God specifically uses evil, but that despite the presence of evil, God still does good. That's why Joseph's life glorified God when he was able to show mercy and kindness to the brothers who had done him so wrong. And Joseph learned a lesson in the process. He could have considered his life over at any point—when he was in the pit, in jail, in exile—but instead he let that suffering sharpen him and draw him closer to the Lord. It was only that long work of being shaped by God that allowed him to show such grace to his brothers when they returned. Joseph could be a blessing to them because he did not allow adversity to be the defining moment of his life.

Adversity. Trials. Tribulation. Call them what you want. They don't have to stay that way. If we learn to push through and go The Extra Mile with God, those hard times can become something. They can become the tools for growth.

* * *

Adrian was doing a great job putting the *Ciclo Vida* tour together, but it was on me to put together a new band. Thankfully, I had Sebas on my team—a sound engineer I'd been working with since I met him at a camp in Bogotá in 2014. Sebas was a true *paisa*—someone from Medellín, Colombia—and he had a ton of contacts and recommendations for me. Better than that, though, Sebas has the kind of faith that is truly infectious. He's one of the most generous people I've ever known—the kind of guy who gives his shoes and even his mattress to anyone who needs it. He trusts God to provide, holds little back for himself, and believes that having a strong faith should always result in making a positive impact on the lives of those around you. Having someone like Sebas on our team only made our foundation stronger.

The band that he helped put together were inexperienced, good-but-not-great musicians, some of whom had never been on a plane before. As soon as we set out for our first concert together just after Easter, I knew they were perfect. After an early flight from Medellín, we had a five-hour drive over rough, winding roads. The new guys were crammed in the back of the minivan, pressed in so tight that they could barely move at all. Not once did any of them complain.

The concert itself was big—big enough for Marcos Witt to be there too. The stage was set in the middle of the venue with the audience wrapping all the way around. It was an impressive sight and the kind of thing that could have left the new guys giddy with either nerves or ego. But again, they were solid throughout, always focused on what God was doing. They understood the vision for what God had called us to, and every time we discussed *Ciclo Vida*, I had an overwhelming sense of gratitude to God that He had brought this band together.

Marcos and I didn't really get any time to talk at the concert, but if we had, I'd have told him this: "I found myself a band of soldiers."

With the band in place, I turned my focus to the other team I needed to put together—the cyclists. A friend from Miami, Pablo, signed up quickly. Paul was totally locked in too, and our mutual friend Essence and her fiancé, Nathan, had agreed to spend their honeymoon joining us on the ride. Pablo is super fit, Essence is a pro enduro mountain biker, and Nathan's a cyclist too, so we were off to a good start. A great start, even, but I wanted to try to get someone from Latin America to join us, and preferably a pro.

I started by talking to the people I'd met in Medellín. As far as I was concerned, we had a pretty good proposition for people: We were going to do well on social media, and even though the ride itself was just over 1,000 miles, the way we were breaking it down meant that for a genuine pro, the physical challenge of *Ciclo Vida* wouldn't be too difficult compared to a pro-only event. The Tour de France covers over 100 miles a day for more than three weeks, while the Vuelta a España averages 149 miles over fourteen days. *Ciclo Vida* broke the 1,000 miles into eighteen riding days, each one averaging out at a much more manageable 60 miles. For an elite road cyclist, it would be relatively easy, but for someone like me, it was a colossal challenge similar to running almost a whole marathon every day for eighteen days in a row.

To make it more appealing to the pros, I was always careful to explain that we were planning on raising up to $100,000 to donate to local nonprofits that were directly changing lives of people in the region. We would have three support vehicles with us on the ride at all times and were offering to cover our riders' food and accommodations throughout the ride. I was even happy to use my air miles to help with transport down to Chile and back from Argentina. In my mind, at least, *Ciclo Vida* was a great opportunity. It was all upside with zero down. How could any pro resist?

I must have been missing something because

even though a few of the locals were interested, nobody was interested enough to say yes.

So I hit Instagram. And I hit it hard. I started messaging every Latin and Latina pro cyclist I could find. I was in full sales mode, emphasizing the positives and doing everything I could to communicate just what a great opportunity this was.

And still, nobody said yes.

So I widened my search. I started reaching out to bike companies and anyone else from the region who I felt could bring something to the ride.

Still nothing.

It was June now, and *Ciclo Vida* was just twelve weeks away. I was starting to stress about it all, thinking that if someone didn't say yes soon, we'd just have to stick with the riders we had. I didn't hate the idea of being an all-American team, but it wasn't my first choice. *Ciclo Vida* was about joining in with what God was already doing in Latin America, and it made sense to me that we ought to have some Latin riders among us.

I had spent hours scrolling and exploring and finding new people to follow, but as soon as I saw

Alice Varela, I stopped. She was everything I had been looking for: a pro cyclist from Venezuela. But that was only half the story. Alice wasn't just any pro on a bike; she was a Paralympic cyclist. Her Instagram account showed her wearing a prosthetic leg as she went about her everyday life, then cycling without it in a velodrome.

I tried my best to figure out her story. It seemed that she'd been involved in an accident and her right leg had been amputated above the knee. I couldn't tell whether her involvement in cycling had started before or after the accident, but it was obvious from her posts that she was refusing to let her disability stop her. She was passionate about inspiring people and encouraging them to persevere through whatever adversity they were facing.

Everything I saw and read about Alice impressed me. I knew that she would be an incredible person to have on the ride—not just for the rest of us cyclists and the team in general, but for those ten audiences we would be playing to along the way. How cool would it be to have Alice come out onstage for five minutes during each concert? I'd encountered so much adversity in all my travels across Latin America and knew that young people would find her inspiring. She could deliver her message of resilience and determination, which would connect deeply with so many people. I loved the idea of being able to hand the microphone to Alice and then encouraging people to place their hope in Jesus. The whole thing could be so powerful.

Alice, however, wasn't so keen.

As soon as I'd stumbled across her account, I had DMed her, but our first conversation wasn't exactly full of positive energy.

> *@evancraft: Hey Alice. I've seen your profile and love what you're doing. I'm organizing a ride from Santiago to Buenos Aires in August to raise money for local charities. I'd love you to join us. Can we talk sometime so that I can tell you more about it?*

She got back to me almost immediately.

@alicevareliita: I've never been out of Venezuela.

It wasn't the worst rejection I'd received so far, so I dug in.

@evancraft: That's okay, Alice. We can book flights for you. Would you want to join us?

@alicevareliita: Maybe. I don't know. I gotta talk to my coach first.

That was it. After those first few messages, there was nothing but silence. Whatever I'd said hadn't been enough to convince Alice, so I gave up and went back to searching anywhere and everywhere for someone else to join us.

One month before the ride was due to start I was looking at my phone when a new post from Alice came up. It was like so many of the others that she had shared—an image of her out riding, eyes locked in determination on the track ahead of her. Below she had written something that perfectly matched the image: "I gotta keep going forward. And I will tell other people that they can do it too. I will tell people that life is still worth living."

I noticed for the first time that she was wearing her Venezuela Paralympic kit, and I started thinking about what life must have been like for her. With inflation at 10,000 percent and the country in the midst of unprecedented social and humanitarian collapse, Venezuela was in the news every week. It was an almost impossible country to live in. People were fleeing to Brazil, to Colombia, to Argentina, to Mexico, and all the way to the US. Life there was so hard that people were willing to risk everything to leave. And yet Alice was still there.

It hit me again just how remarkable Alice was. Over the previous weeks I had looked at hundreds, maybe even thousands of other cyclists' Instagram accounts, and none of them had anything like Alice's power to connect and inspire. She was perfect. But she was still silent.

I messaged her again.

@evancraft: Hey Alice. I'd love it if you could join us on the ride. Are you sure you can't go with us?

This time, her reply wasn't immediate.

It took days before she got back to me. But when she did, her tone had changed.

@alicevareliita: Could I bring my cycling partner?

For just a brief moment I could feel myself flirting with the idea of saying no. Whoever this cycling partner was, I didn't need anyone freeloading. We were trying to raise as much money as possible, and paying for another set of flights and accommodation was going to cost us. But then I thought about it from her perspective and saw how weird the whole thing must appear: A totally random American guy makes contact out of the blue and offers to fly you to another country to take part in some wild cycle event. If she wasn't suspicious, she probably should have been. Asking to bring someone along with her wasn't her being a diva; it was her being totally sensible and smart. It made me like her even more.

So the next day I hit reply.

@evancraft: Yes! We'd love to have you both on the team!

Alice got back to me immediately. She was beyond happy, and she sent me a link to her cycling partner's profile. I clicked on it right away. Alex was another Paralympic athlete—a young guy whose right leg had been amputated below the knee.

Chapter Four

Expect the Unexpected

I don't remember how old I was when I first heard the name Reinhard Bonnke. I guess it was my dad who first introduced the stranger to my world, but I have no memory of where I was at the time, or—other than a few details—what it was he told me about him. But what I do remember is exactly what I felt.

I felt awe. Excitement. And a cast-iron certainty that Reinhard Bonnke was doing something that God smiled upon—the kind of thing that I wanted to see for myself.

If you don't know anything about Bonnke, you need to remedy that as soon as possible and go read his autobiography, *Living a Life of Fire*. He was a German-American evangelist known as the Billy Graham of Africa, and he regularly preached to crowds in excess of 150,000. Over the five decades of his ministry he saw over seventy million people become Christians. As well as preaching the gospel, he followed Jesus' lead and encouraged those who were sick to receive prayer for healing. And the way God healed people was astounding.

The blind saw. The deaf heard. People who were crippled walked again. Tumors vanished. The dead were raised back to life. The holy chaos of the book of Acts was unleashed on the crowds of people who were desperately hungry to see God at work. In other words, it was exactly what the Bible tells us we should be experiencing. It was both totally ordinary and completely extraordinary at the same time.

I've been a fan of Reinhard Bonnke and his ministry ever since I heard about him. But of all the stories about his life and partnership with God, my favorite isn't set in one of his tent meetings. It's not even about anyone getting healed.

Bonnke was a twelve-year-old boy living near a small port in Germany. He liked being by the water, especially playing in the mud when the tide was out and looking up at the cargo vessels that listed on their sides, held fast by the mud and silt. It amazed him that these ships weighing hundreds of tons could ever be picked up and moved, but within hours the tide would come in and the ships would be floating once again, up against the dock. Bonnke would lean his back against the heavy metal railings, place a foot on the ship, and push with all his might. And whenever he did, the ship would move.

"When we obey the Word of God," Bonnke said, "the tide comes in. The immovable becomes movable. The incurable becomes curable. And the impossible is possible."

* * *

In early August 2018, Reinhard Bonnke and the power of God's Spirit were on my mind a lot. I realized that the restlessness that had led me to dream up *Ciclo Vida* wasn't just a dissatisfaction with the sense that life had become a little too comfortable in places. It was a symptom of the fact that I didn't feel as though I'd been overawed by God of late—a situation that was 100 percent on me, not God. I hadn't seen God in action because I hadn't been looking for Him in action. I'd been so busy doing life as normal that I hadn't been pushing against the ships at high tide. I'd lost the awe and the excitement because I hadn't been searching for it.

The closer I got to the start of the ride, the more clearly I saw it. This was an opportunity to stop doing life as normal and put myself back in the place where I had no choice other than to rely on God. It was a chance to start over, to get back to the way things used to be. It was the chance to take some risks and be wide-eyed and eager to see God at work.

As I hauled my bike and way too many kilos of excess luggage out of the airport in Santiago, Chile, on August 25, it was game on. There were four days before the ride would begin, six days before our first concert, and at least forty-eight hours before anyone else from *Ciclo Vida* was due to arrive. It was the calm before the storm, the chance for me to wander out onto the riverbed at low tide, like the twelve-year-old Reinhard Bonnke, and marvel at what God was going to do.

Already I was aware how much we needed Him.

In the previous weeks there had been some unwelcome reports of financial turbulence in Argentina. Things are often chaotic there, but even by the usual standards, this news was worrying. Inflation was three times its usual rate, soy crops had failed, and the IMF had just given the country the largest loan in its history. Everything was in turmoil and the value of the peso was dropping lower and lower with every passing month. Some of the churches we were planning on playing at were already getting worried about covering costs, and the fact that the peso was worth less now than it was when we'd started planning the ride was putting an extra load of pressure on our budget.

It was worrying, but it also made things simpler: Without God, we were in trouble.

From the airport in Santiago, I drove west along the highway to our starting base in the coastal town of Viña del Mar. It's a beautiful place, dominated by both its strong music culture and the brooding, swelling Pacific Ocean at its flank—a perfect backdrop for the beginning of an adventure like ours. I was feeling fitter than at any point in my life and was also getting a nice payoff from having spent all that time at altitude back in Medellín. When I put my bike together and rode for just a few miles after I arrived, I felt like Superman. Added to that, it was winter in the Southern Hemisphere, and due to being a good distance south of the equator, the temperature was considerably cooler than Medellín. The air was cool and the skies were clear. To me it felt as though everything inside and outside of me was saying, *Let's go!*

The team had grown and now stood at a total of eighteen people. With Alice and her cycling partner, Alex, on board, there were seven of us riders, as well as the band and crew, which included Adrian, Sebas, and a small team of videographers. I wanted to be there to welcome them all, so I spent my first three days in Chile driving the seventy miles each way between Viña del Mar and the airport to collect people and bring them back to the base. The videographers, who had flown in from Guatemala and El Salvador, impressed me right away. It was good to be reunited with Paul and Pablo again, and to see Essence and meet her husband, Nathan. It was clear that the other riders were just as pumped about the challenge ahead of us as I was, and by the looks of them, they were in great physical shape.

There was one extra person flying in for *Ciclo Vida* who I was especially excited to greet: my older sister, Lindy. She's a medical doctor who specializes in trauma, so even though we hoped that she'd not be needed to do anything medical on the ride, it was good to have her join us. She was the extra insurance you know you don't need that you take out anyway at the rental counter. By having her skills and expertise with us, I hoped it meant we wouldn't have any need for her medical training at all.

That wasn't the only reason for her being with us. Lindy had just gone through a breakup and was at one of those points in her life when she just needed to hit pause, pack a bag, and get thousands of miles away from everything. She needed to decompress, unwind, and forget all about life back home.

There were even more reasons to be glad to have her with us. Lindy had never been to Latin America before and had never seen me play live. Having my big sister there with me at such a significant time was a bonus. And best of all, I had the sense that God might be up to something. Lindy and church hadn't gotten on too well for many years, but the fact that she was willing to come down to Chile and join us while we rode and played and prayed and talked about God *a lot* made me deeply happy.

There I was, in the mud, looking at a stationary ship. Only God could make her move.

"Hey, Bible thumper," she said when we hugged at Arrivals.

"Good to see you, heathen."

Lindy took a step back and looked at me carefully, like she was studying a CT scan of my brain.

Now, fashion and I have always had a solid enough relationship—at least, that's the way I see it. I did the skater look when I was a tween, flirted with a more nerdy thing as I matured, and then found my groove in my twenties. The way I see it, I'm not the best dressed, but I'm not the worst either.

Lindy, however, had other thoughts. And maybe she was right. At that moment, a couple of days before the ride, I wasn't looking my best. I was looking like a bike nerd. I was wearing sweats, some very comfortable footwear, and, I'm guessing, some kind of technical top that we amateur cyclists have way too much affection for.

"Yeah," she said, her critical eye resting on my hi-vis, moisture-wicking top. "You're never getting married. You know that, don't you?"

* * *

My last trip from Viña del Mar to the airport was different. On all the others I'd felt excited, especially as we'd be cycling along the same highway at the start of the ride. I'd let my mind drift to what I imagined it would feel like with the seven of us riding in a perfect peloton, shielding each other from the wind, eating up mile after mile. It was a good daydream, one I couldn't wait to experience in real time.

But on my last drive in from the coast, things

were different. It was early in the morning and the sun was not yet up.

Nerves are a regular feature of my life. There are certain feelings that I get in the last half hour before any concert starts. I get butterflies, feel anxious, and count down the minutes until the music will start and I can finally relax. There was a time when nerves would trouble me, and I would think of them as an unwelcome distraction. But over the years I've learned to accept the nerves, to lean into them and appreciate them for what they are—signs that I'm doing something that feels like a risk. Something that matters. Something that could go so badly wrong if my head and heart are in the wrong place, but that also could go so right if I step aside and get out of God's way. Feeling nervous isn't something that repels me from the action; it draws me closer. I guess that's another part of what Marcos was trying to communicate when he asked me about being an artist or a soldier. Soldiers are trained to run toward risk. As an artist, it can be tempting to avoid it.

I was nervous on this last drive because this was the one where I was finally going to meet Alice and her cycling partner, Alex. *Ciclo Vida* was a risk, and it was something that mattered. I was determined that I was going to do everything I could to keep out of God's way. I was going to do everything possible to allow the ride to fulfill its potential. I was determined to be a soldier, not an artist.

Bringing Alice and Alex along was also a risk, and it mattered so much to me that it went well for them. As I was heading to meet them, the responsibility of it all hit me. The other riders all came from the US. We were all able-bodied. We saw the world from similar perspectives, and I knew that we were approaching the ride with a shared sense of confidence.

With Alice and Alex, it was different. I knew their names and I knew Alice's cell number, which I had used to PayPal her money to cover the excess luggage fee for bringing their bikes with them from Venezuela. All I really knew about Alex and Alice was how different they were from the rest of us. The amount I didn't know about them—their backgrounds, their outlooks on life, their stories, their current life situations, their fitness, their ability to ride as amputees, their faith—it was colossal. Yet here I was, about to bring them along on a ride that I was already personally nervous about. I was the fittest I'd ever been, but while riding up and down that highway so many times, I'd noticed the first whispers of doubt rise up within me. Could I really push myself for a thousand miles from coast to coast, crossing the Andes in the process? Could Alice? Could Alex? Had I let myself get way too excited on this one—carried away by something I'd seen on Instagram that I would come to regret?

I pulled into the parking lot and made the familiar journey to Arrivals.

I spotted them immediately. They looked tired. Maybe a little anxious too.

But it was what they didn't have that worried me. Neither of them had much luggage, just a backpack and standard carry-on that seemed way too small for a monthlong trip, nothing like the mountains of gear that everyone else had brought with them. There were no bikes anywhere near them. And Alice was on crutches with no sign of a prosthetic leg. The right pant leg of her jeans was tied in a knot where her knee had once been.

I went up and introduced myself. "I'm so glad to finally meet you both. And I'm grateful that you both agreed to come. Are you still waiting for some luggage? The bikes will be at the oversized counter over there."

"No, this is all the luggage we have," said Alice, her voice high-pitched, loud, and machine-gun fast. "And the bikes! It was terrible. They wouldn't let us check the bikes at Caracas. They said we had to pay with *bolívares*, not a transfer. It was 3:00 a.m. and nowhere was open for us to get the cash. So we had to leave them behind." She paused, glancing at Alex. "I'm sorry."

She said the words quietly, cautiously, the way someone tests the ice on a frozen lake to see if it is strong enough to hold them. She glanced at Alex again. He tensed. Put a hand on her shoulder.

"Don't worry," I said, shelving my disappointment and being careful to look them both in the eyes and smile. "Seriously, it's all going to be fine. It's just great that you're both here."

We made our way back to the parking lot, with me trying to figure out how we were going to get our hands on two quality road bikes the right size at short notice. I had a spare bike back in Medellín that would probably do for Alice. Getting it down to Santiago was possible, as there were a couple of guys in the band who were due to fly out from Medellín in a couple of days. If I could get the guard to let them into my apartment, they could pack it up and bring it with them. It would mean Alice missing the first day of the ride, but it was better than nothing. For Alex, we'd just have to put the word out in Santiago and hope that someone would be able to loan us one.

Once we were driving, I asked the question that had been brewing within me since I first saw them at Arrivals. Something told me that Alex was still trying to figure out whether I could be trusted, so I made sure to keep my tone light and easy.

"So, Alice," I said, looking back at her in the rearview mirror. "How come you don't have the prosthetic that you've got in all those Instagram pictures?"

She shifted in her seat. "It's not mine. I mean, it was mine for a time. The government told me that they would give me a prosthetic and they promised to fit it for me. They even had me take all those photos with it. I was so excited. It was going to change my life. But it wasn't possible to use it."

"How come?"

"They never did fit it properly. It was two inches longer than my other leg, which meant it was really uncomfortable and I couldn't do anything in it. Eventually they just took it back."

"You're kidding! Your government would do that?"

Both Alex and Alice shot me the same look. A look that said, *Why are you in any way surprised?*

I thought about the difference between the picture I'd built up in my mind of Alice's life, and the reality. I'd assumed that with her prosthetic she was able to do almost anything that she had been able to do before she lost her leg. Now I wasn't so sure. And I wasn't so sure that the challenge of *Ciclo Vida* was limited to her time on the bike. Using crutches meant that she'd need help carrying her stuff around, and that stairs would be a problem.

Alex must have been reading my mind. "She's fast on those crutches, though. Fast enough to catch me and give me a whack if I get out of line."

Alice leaned forward and aimed a playful slap at Alex's head. Something told me they were more than just cycling partners.

We drove for awhile without saying much more. Then Alice spoke up.

"How many other Paralympic athletes are on *Ciclo Vida*?"

"It's just you two," I said. There was another glance between them, and I suddenly realized that I wasn't the only one who'd made some wrong assumptions. They were clearly expecting there to be others on the ride, and the news caught them off guard. I tried to remember if I'd given the impression that there were others with physical disabilities on the ride, but I was pretty sure I hadn't. "Is that going to be okay with you?"

Alice inhaled and searched for the words. "No. It's okay. But, Evan, I'm going to be slower than you. Alex has full use of his quads on both legs, so he'll be fine. He'll keep up. But my amputation is above the knee, so I've got half the power that the rest of you have. I can't do hills. So really, the question is one for you to answer. Is it going to be okay with you?"

"Yes," I said. I meant it with every ounce of my being. "Of course it's okay. I really believe that God brought you two here to be a part of this. We'll do whatever we need to make things work for you both."

The conversation shifted to the ride itself, and we went over the details again. Despite the problems with Alice's and Alex's bikes and the increased financial pressure caused by the monetary crisis in Argentina, the plan for the ride had remained solid from the moment we'd locked in the route and the concerts.

"The only variable is the weather," I said. "And I'm checking a ton of forecasts daily. They all say there's no rain, no wind, and no real change in temperature. It's ideal riding weather, so as long as we hit our mileage target each day, we'll be fine."

We were just coming into Viña del Mar when we got our first sight of the ocean. Alice was suddenly lost under its spell and stared at it out the window. After a few moments of silence, I asked Alex the question that I'd been wanting to ask since meeting him at the airport.

"Can I ask you how you lost your leg?"

"Sure." He smiled and reached down and tapped the prosthetic that started just past his knee. "I was on my motorbike, making a left turn on a road in my neighborhood. I'd made that turn hundreds of times before and never had a problem. But this time a guy in a truck was trying to escape the police, and he came around the corner too fast for me to do anything. He drove right at me, catching my bike and sending me flying."

Alex paused. I said nothing even though I had a hundred questions inside.

"I remember everything. I was lying on the ground, looking over at my bike a few feet away. It was destroyed, mangled in a way that no mechanic could fix. As I was staring at it, I was aware of the mess around me. There was blood and bits of my jeans and other things spread out in a line about ten feet away from me. I looked closely, followed the trail that led right to where I was lying. It was my leg, crushed and lifeless. I didn't do anything. I just stared. It looked so odd.

"Suddenly I could hear someone shouting. I felt

a pair of strong hands grab hold of me and drag me away. They'd just got me to the other side of the street when my bike exploded.

"Next thing I knew, I woke up in hospital. I was in surgery. They were operating on me, amputating my leg, but they didn't have any anesthetic to give me. They were pulling on tendons and nerves and I could feel every single thing they did to me…" His voice trailed off.

"I can't imagine how painful that must have been for you, Alex." I glanced at him. He had tears in his eyes.

"I was screaming, '*Somebody kill me!*' It was so hard, believe me. I wouldn't wish pain like that on anyone."

We drove a little farther.

"They operated for two hours like that. I was begging them to kill me, but they weren't listening. They just kept on working, amputating my leg. And it wasn't just the pain that tortured me. I knew that without a leg I'd be a cripple. I wouldn't walk or work ever again. I'd be a burden on my family. I'd end up like one of those guys on the street, dragging myself around in a wheelchair, asking people for money. Who would notice me? Who would love me? I wasn't just losing my leg; I was losing my life. I didn't want that. Not for me. Not for my family. So I decided that as soon as I got out of hospital, I'd get a hold of a gun and shoot myself."

Alex was crying now. Alice was leaning forward, her hand on his shoulder. She was crying too.

We were just about to pull up to the house in Viña del Mar, and I told them we'd be there in a couple of minutes. Alex's tears stopped and he wiped his face.

"So what happened?" I asked. "How did you survive?"

"For a long time it seemed that killing myself was the only option open to me. But somehow I didn't do it. Maybe I was too depressed, because I was just sitting at home, doing nothing. And then a friend visited and said he had a present for me. I followed him outside and saw a pedal bike. I thought it was a sick joke at first, but he told me that the bike was mine, that he was sure I could ride it, and that he thought it would be good for me. I tried it and found that he was right. I could ride, even without my leg.

From then on, I had the strength to keep going."

I had only known Alice and Alex for a couple of hours, but as I showed them into the house where the team was staying and introduced them to their fellow riders, I wanted everyone to know how great they were. They were tough and resilient in ways that brought tears to my eyes. They had both experienced more loss and tragedy than I could imagine. They could talk about the pain in their past, but they didn't seem to be tormented by it. They came from a country that clearly wasn't functioning, yet they were prepared to take a risk on a stranger like me and sign up for this crazy adventure. They had more freedom, more strength, and more courage than a lot of people I knew back home.

The rest of the team was just finishing breakfast when Alex, Alice, and I walked in. As they were being introduced to everyone, they were both eyeing the food on the table—a couple of plates still racked with croissants, some ham, and some cheese.

"You guys must be hungry," I said. "You should help yourselves."

They didn't need telling twice. Alice and Alex loaded their plates with two of everything, and Alex took a few extra croissants and put them in his bag.

"Lunch is going to be here in about three hours," I said, in case they thought we were heading off or were looking at a late one.

Alex looked at me like I'd just told him there would be two moons in the sky that night. "Really?"

"Really. And dinner will be at seven tonight. Then breakfast tomorrow, just like today. We'll feed you up real good. Gotta give you the energy for all those calories we're going to be burning on the ride."

Alice laughed, but Alex just looked back at the table of food and shook his head. "I've never seen so much food," he said. "Never seen anything like it."

There's always been a part of me that wants to be God's hero. If I see someone I think I can help, I want to go all in and fix everything right there, right then. It's good to help, but that help has to be sustainable and it has to be what the person needs. Over the years I've learned to temper that desire with wisdom.

I spent much of the afternoon digging deep for

wisdom. I was so stirred by the way Alice had been treated by her government, by the torment Alex had been through, and by the fact that both of them saw food as a luxury. My knee-jerk reaction was to try to find a way to finance their lives and allow them to never be hungry again. But I knew that was just me rushing ahead too far, too fast. It was me acting in my own strength, forgetting to lean wholly on God.

I needed to look and see which way God was moving, not try to instigate something in my own strength. I needed to follow His lead, not try to take charge myself.

* * *

It's funny, but that day I collected Alice and Alex from the airport was full of potential frustrations. The fact that they turned up without their bikes was a major problem, and Alice's lack of a prosthetic and her confession about how much slower she would be had a major impact on the ride. Even the thing about food was an unexpected difference that I'd never considered, and it left me wondering what else about their lives and expectations I wasn't aware of. But all those questions and points of difference were essential to what came next. They pressed pause. They made me stop. They reminded me that without God, *Ciclo Vida* was nothing.

Planning is good. Having a strategy that we hope will lead to success is great. Being prepared and well trained and ready to take on the challenge ahead is the hallmark of clear thinking and dedication.

But when we get so locked into our own strategies, plans, and plays, we can forget the truth. Like Reinhard Bonnke pushing on those heavy iron ships when they were stuck in the mud, we can forget the only ingredient for transformation that is truly essential: God's power.

There's a story in the Old Testament that rings so true on this.

After forty years of wandering around the wilderness, Joshua was chosen as the strong leader to take on Moses' mantle and finally deliver the Israelites to the promised land. He had gathered his army and was prepared to attack the city of Jericho when an angel appeared before him.

> And Joshua went to him and said to him, "Are you for us, or for our adversaries?"
>
> And he said, "No; but I am the commander of the army of the LORD. Now I have come." And Joshua fell on his face to the earth and worshiped. (Joshua 5:13–14)

For Joshua, this battle was about the Israelites against the Canaanites, and his perspective had become warped. Was God on his side? It's the wrong question. This was God's battle, and the real question was whether Joshua was on God's side. He was told to take off his shoes (v. 15), a clear reminder that we fight on God's terms, not our own.

We need to find the right balance between action and trust. A lot of times, when our plans run aground, it's a perfect opportunity to stop and check in again with God. Have we taken a little too much ownership of things? Are we forgetting whose battle we're really fighting? Have we gotten a little too caught up in our programs and started treating people poorly for the sake of ministry?

Much of the time, in my life at least, God's message isn't ever, *Hey, Evan, nice job with the planning. Why don't you take it from here?* It's usually, *Evan, you need to expect the unexpected.* He knows that's the best way to keep my eyes locked on Him.

* * *

Later that night, as I was getting ready to head to bed, I found Lindy sitting alone.

"You okay?"

She closed her eyes and stretched her arms out in front of her, like I'd just reminded her to do her armchair yoga. "Great." She smiled. "Really great."

"And it's okay with you that everyone's talking in Spanish? You don't feel left out?"

"I can follow along pretty good. What about you? You feel okay about tomorrow?"

I made a face. In less than twelve hours *Ciclo Vida* would begin. Physically, I was ready. Mentally, I was wired. A part of me wanted to skip the sleep and get straight on and start riding there and then.

We sat in silence for a while.

There was a time when we were kids when she and I didn't get along too well. It was just the usual brother-sister stuff, and we grew out of it soon enough. But sitting there, knowing that my big sister was with me, I felt like a kid again in the best possible way. As long as she was there, everything was going to be okay.

"You know," she said, "you've got a problem with Alex."

My warm feeling cooled. "What do you mean?"

She sat up and looked me in the eye. The big sister was still there, but so, too, was the medic with eight years of training behind her.

"His prosthetic. Have you seen how it has tape on it?"

"Yeah."

"If it had been properly fitted, he shouldn't need tape. But he clearly does, so all this cycling could cause rashes. If they get infected, he could be in trouble."

"Trouble how?"

"It depends. But if it got really bad, he could lose more of his leg."

Chapter Five

The Worst of Evan Craft

I woke up ready. I felt great. I had no aches, no pains, nothing that would hold me back. My body was full of energy, my confidence high after months of training. I felt even better as soon as I checked my phone. I discovered that a local pastor had agreed to lend Alex a Trek bike for the duration of the ride. Better still, a couple of the guys in my band had messaged me to confirm that they'd been to my apartment in Medellín, gotten a hold of my spare bike, and were bringing it with them when they flew later that day.

It was the perfect start. Within an hour, it got even better.

There weren't enough beds for us all at Pastor Rodrigo's house, which was our designated base, so Alice and Alex had slept at another home nearby with a couple who were friends of Pastor Rodrigo's. The wife brought Alice and Alex over to join us all for breakfast, and as soon as the three of them walked in, it was obvious that they were already getting along well. They were locked in conversation as if they'd known each other for years.

After we finished our early breakfast, Pastor Rodrigo sat down next to me and told me how glad he was that Alice and Alex had connected with the couple. "They lost their son to cancer recently. It's been so hard for them. But last night they stayed up late talking and crying with those two. I think it was really healing for them to listen to Alice and Alex talk about what it means to lose so much but to find a way to keep on with life."

My heart was full.

Alice's honesty and positivity had been what had jumped out at me when I first came across her on Instagram. I'd had a hunch that she was the perfect person for the ride, but seeing her in action like this was even better. And we hadn't even climbed onto our bikes yet.

My optimism was way high.

The plan for the first day of the ride was simple. After an early breakfast we were going to head down to the waterfront in Viña del Mar, take a few photos, do a couple of interviews, and then set off at nine thirty, ten at the latest. We'd planned on starting out strong on that first day, and we were hoping to cover seventy miles and reach the outskirts of Santiago. Once we'd hit that distance, we'd load up into the support vehicles and return to Viña del Mar for another night, staying at the home of Pastor Rodrigo and his friends. The next day we'd drive back out to Santiago and pick up where we left off.

Those plans hit an early bump when it became clear that as well as not having their bikes, Alice and Alex also needed some essential riding gear. It took a while to track some down, but we did eventually. There was another delay with the bike that Alex was borrowing. It didn't turn up as early as I hoped it would, so by the time we finally got down to the waterfront, it was past eleven o'clock in the morning.

The interviews took us until way past noon. By then, I was starting to get a little on edge. I wanted to be on the road, putting some miles behind us so that we could reach our destination well ahead of sunset.

There was yet another break while the video guys were setting up their drone. That's when I noticed Alice. She was standing away from the rest of the riders, staring at the ocean.

"Are you okay?" It dawned on me then that she might not be. The band weren't due to arrive with my spare bike until later the next day, so Alice was going to have to miss out on the first two days of the ride. For a pro like her, it was bound to be frustrating.

She carried on looking at the water. "It's so beautiful."

"What? Oh, yeah." I glanced at the waves. They were flat and a little gray. Coming from California, I wasn't so sure I could see the uniqueness or the beauty myself.

"I can't believe I'm here, Evan. I can't believe I'm actually in Chile, and that I'm at the ocean. I've never seen it before."

"Chile?"

"No. The ocean."

It took a moment for her words to sink in, but when they did, I was stunned. "You mean you've never seen the ocean before? But you live in Caracas. It's like twenty miles from the coast."

She shrugged. "Maybe. But we're not allowed to leave the Paralympic compound unless we have permission, so it doesn't matter how close it is."

"Wait. They don't let you out?"

Alice looked at me and shrugged, like she was confirming something so obvious she assumed that everyone knew it.

Like everyone, I understood that life in Venezuela was tough. I knew that almost 95 percent of people lived in poverty, and that by whatever measure you judged it, the country was barely functioning. I'd known that people were trapped by poverty, but for an athlete to effectively be held captive?

Alice's eyes were back on the ocean. "We get food at the Paralympic center, so we're in a better situation than most people. But they also make a lot of promises that they don't keep."

"What kind of promises?"

"Oh, you know. They tell us that we're going to travel to compete in an international Paralympic event. They even buy us tickets sometimes, but something always goes wrong at the last minute and the trip is canceled. Once it almost happened. We got up at 5:00 a.m. ready to go to the airport, but the car never came and our tickets were declined. We can't trust them, but what can we do? It's not like there's a better future out there for us in Venezuela. The Paralympic center is the best we can hope for."

We both watched the waves for a while. In the background I could hear a drone buzzing, but I didn't look back.

"That's why I can't believe we were given permission to travel and that we're really here. Every other good thing we've ever been told about has turned out to be a lie. There was a part of us that thought this would be the same. But you didn't let us down. We're here. Looking at the ocean. About to start the ride."

Someone called my name and yelled that they were ready for the shot. But Alice wasn't done talking.

"Evan, we don't want to go back to Venezuela. Will you help us stay?"

* * *

We must have spent over an hour taking photos and shooting some video. I appreciated the fact that the guys wanted to do their job well, but according to the schedule, we should have been on the road three hours ago. We were late, and I was not happy.

The guys wanted to get one more shot of us all walking down to the beach in turn and dipping our tires into the Pacific. It was an important shot, and I didn't want to miss it, so I hurried up and waited.

What Alice had said made me nervous. The more I thought about it, the more I could understand why they wouldn't want to return to Venezuela, but I was troubled by the idea of them making such a big decision when they'd only been out of their homeland for twenty-four hours. I wanted to help them, but the responsibility felt like a weight that I couldn't carry at that moment. Plenty of people left

Venezuela, but Alice and Alex had nothing—no job, no money, and no contacts in Chile. They were way more vulnerable than someone in perfect physical health. Could they really cope with life as migrants in a foreign land? Did I really want to be the person who helped them get out of Venezuela, only for them to discover that life as a refugee was even worse?

* * *

The shots were all done, and I was ready. But even then we couldn't go, as one of the three support vehicles had gone off to run an errand. We all stood around awhile, some riders choosing to get some last-minute snacks, while others, like me, pacing back and forth.

Finally, at 2:00 p.m., the vehicle returned, and we were ready to go. I was wired and buzzing like I'd just been unplugged from the power grid, and as soon as we clipped in and pushed off into the streets of Viña del Mar, I was out front, setting the kind of pace that matched my mood.

The first half mile was easy, just flat domestic

streets lined with parked cars leading away from the coast.

Then we hit the hill.

It was nothing compared to what I was used to back in Medellín, and hardly any steeper than the one I'd encountered on my first ride in Pasadena with Paul. But after two miles of the ride, I was struggling. My head began bobbing from side to side, I took short breaths, and my stomach was full of nerves. If I was feeling like this at two miles, how was I going to cope with the other 1,200? I was kidding myself that the ride was possible.

I could hear other riders close to me and looked back to see Alex. He gave me a smile. "It's always tough at the start. All those miles ahead. All those mountains."

I tried to think of something to say, but I had nothing.

"One mile at a time, Evan. That's all you've got to do."

The hill leveled out soon enough and I gradually felt myself settle. We turned onto the highway—the same one that I had driven along every time I had gone to the airport—but on a bike it was unfamiliar and strange. I'd not noticed the debris and general trash that littered the side of the road, and I hadn't gotten a sense of how chaotic the cars and trucks were, weaving in and out of each other all the time.

The video guys were loving it. The drone was doing its thing above us, and the guys were crammed into one of the vehicles, making repeated passes next to us. They had the minivan door wide open and the camera guy was leaning out, shooting what I guessed would be epic-looking tracking shots.

Something about the video guys and the wild traffic must have rubbed off on us, because soon I looked up and saw that we were spread out over at least one hundred feet. We weren't riding as a peloton but as six total strangers.

Ten miles in, Paul surged ahead, took the lead, and waved for everyone to pull over on the side of the road.

"Listen," he said, his voice full of authority. "We can't ride like this. We stick together as a peloton, right? That means there's one person in the front; they're the lead. We all follow their pace, and we don't leave people behind. If you're in the back and you're going to fall behind, you yell out. The rest pass the message forward and the peloton slows down. It's on the leader to call out for debris, and it's on everyone else to keep in real close to the rider in front. You got that?"

We nodded, and I translated for Alex just to be sure that he was getting it. He gave me a look that told me he was thinking the same thing as Paul.

We set out again, this time trying to bunch up close and ride in formation like the pros do in order to minimize wind resistance. Paul was at the front, setting a steady pace and calling out from time to time when there was debris or some other obstacle that the rest of us needed to be aware of. As the least experienced rider of all, I was a little freaked out by having to keep my front wheel less than four inches from the rider in front's back wheel. But the rest of them were all solid, confident riders who'd done this plenty of times before. All I needed to do was keep my place and match their pace.

Riding like that allowed me to get a sense of what the other bikers were like. Alex's prosthetic didn't appear to bother him at all, and he was clearly putting plenty of power through both his legs without any problem. Essence was showing us that women can be tough to beat, and Pablo was demonstrating the benefits of having trained with pros in Colombia. I knew all about Paul's fitness from our rides in California, but it was Nathan who surprised me the most. He wasn't as bulky as Paul, but he was tall, lean, and extremely athletic. We were all going at the same speed, some of us having to put in more effort than others. But for Nathan, it was as if he were hardly working at all. When he took over for Paul at the front, even though he was taking the full force of the wind, Nathan was still hardly needing to work at all.

Forty minutes in, Nathan tensed up and yelled, "Flat!"

The whole peloton slowed and pulled up at the side of the road. It was unlucky, but not exactly unexpected. While Nathan took his wheel off and replaced his inner tube, the rest of us took a moment to have a drink and try to figure out what nickname we should give Nathan: the blonde, athletic, easy-going medical student.

"Thor," we all said at exactly the same time.

It stuck immediately.

Thirty minutes later we were back on the road.

Another ten minutes after that, there was another shout from a rider and another flat tire to change. This time it was Alex who'd run over something sharp, and this time, we weren't so relaxed about it all.

"Unbelievable," I said. "Two flats within a half hour. Have you ever seen that happen before?"

Nobody had.

We stood and watched and waited as Alex changed his tire. He was a little quicker than Nathan, but the minutes felt longer and slower than they had on the previous stop. There was no joking around this time and not much in the way of easy conversation. Just six frustrated cyclists standing around, kicking at the small pebbles, screws, and other trash that littered the side of the road.

I checked my watch. Did some calculations. We had covered twenty miles in an hour and a half. When we'd been cycling and not changing tires, we'd averaged thirteen miles per hour. At this rate, it was going to take us another five hours to reach Santiago. It was already three thirty in the afternoon, which gave us around two and a half hours of light to ride by. There was no way we were going to make it. There was no way we were even going to come close. And if the rest of the ride was going to be like this—with eight hours spent on the bike—there was no way I could hope to be able to do the concerts in the evening as well.

Alex finished up and we clipped in and rode off again, this time with Pablo at the head of the peloton. My mind was a swirl of miles and times as I tried to figure out how far we could realistically hope to get by the end of the day, and how we'd need to adjust the following days' targets as a result. It was not the kind of situation I had imagined us being in on this first day, and it left me frustrated.

I was also starting to feel lightheaded and cranky from not having eaten since nine o'clock. Some of the riders had snacked while we'd been waiting to start the ride at Viña del Mar, but not me. And now I was starting to regret it, especially as we were picking up our pace. The prospect of cranking out another couple of hours riding like this was not good.

I had my phone set up so that I could call the support team as I rode. Adrian was in one of the vehicles, and the plan for that first day was that he'd go source some lunch and meet wherever and whenever we wanted to stop to eat. I checked with the other riders, and we all agreed that now was a great time to take on some more fuel.

Trouble was, Adrian wasn't answering his phone.

I tried again. Same result.

I called one of the other guys instead. It was hard to make myself heard above the road noise and keep myself in the right position in the peloton, so I could only talk in short, half-shouted bursts.

"Where's Adrian?"

"Oh, hey. He went to get food."

"Okay. Is he back?"

"Not yet. He's been a while though."

"How long?"

"A couple of hours already. We're trying to call him but can't get through."

For a moment I wondered if something was wrong, but I pushed the thought from my mind. "We need food now. We're burning calories here."

A few minutes passed and then the familiar shout of "FLAT!" returned.

Essence had been caught this time, and the whole peloton groaned in frustration.

"Are you kidding me?!"

"How are we going to get to Buenos Aires in a month if we can't even go five miles without getting a flat?"

We pulled over to the side and watched as Essence got to work.

I tried Adrian again, but the call rang without him picking up. When I hung up I realized that most of the other riders were looking at me. I stood for a while and stared at the road ahead. This was not how I'd expected the first day to go.

"I'm thinking," I said to the other riders, my head really starting to spin now and my stomach starting to ache, "that we really need to eat. It looks like there's a garage on that off-ramp up ahead. Let me go ahead while Essence is changing her tire here. I'll see if I can find some food for us."

They agreed and I set off alone.

Good news: The garage was open and had a shop that sold food.

Bad news: The food was limited to a handful of old, stale cheese sandwiches. I had a little money on me, but not enough, so I bought what I could, then waited out front for the vehicles to arrive.

Between the hunger, the stress, and the frustration, I was feeling the urge to freak out just a little bit. Besides Adrian, there was one other person I wanted to talk to on the phone. My dad.

"Hey, Evan. How's it going?"

I let out a long sigh. "Good, I guess. Alice and Alex are great, and we're on the way. But it's been a crazy day. Lots of flats."

"Well, you know these things happen. Expect the unexpected, right, son?"

We talked awhile longer. Just hearing his voice was enough to take the edge off my stress.

A few minutes after we'd finished talking, the rest of the riders pulled in, followed by two of the vehicles. There was no sign of Adrian.

We pulled together the cash to buy the rest of the sandwiches and stood around.

"I'm sorry," I said to the riders as they washed down stale bread and cheese with what was left in their water bottles. "This isn't what the rest of the ride is going to be like. I was hoping that—"

A car pulled off the ramp and swung into the garage. It was Adrian. He got out, smiling, and held up a small shopping bag.

"Anyone hungry?"

I looked at him, confused. "What happened?"

"Oh man," he said in his usual bright and airy way. "It's crazy trying to find anything around here. It's taken me hours to find something that everyone will like. But look, I got PB and J and some bread. I think it might not be the freshest bread ever, but it's all calories, right?"

The hunger left me. The stress about reaching Santiago vanished. The frustration about the state of the road and the three flat tires we'd been plagued by disappeared. And in their place was pure, raw anger. The kind that takes over your mouth, bypasses

Celebrating the start of Ciclovida at La Moneda (the Chilean presidential palace).

Alex helping Alice climb the Andes mountains in Chile.

Nathan and Alex helping Alice.

ABOVE: Paul at the top of the Chilean mountains.

RIGHT: I made it to the border of Argentina and Chile, 12,000 feet high.

Above: We climbed past thirty-two switchbacks up the mountain.

Left: Paul's helmet after the crash with Alice.

Riding towards a storm from Córdoba to Villa María.

ABOVE:
What was supposed to be the "easy" part.

RIGHT:
Listening to music and praying God would make a way for us to get the prosthetics.

ABOVE: Performing in Argentina.

LEFT: Alex and Alice try on their new prosthetics with Dr. Mario.

Alex rode on stage with his new prosthetic in Córdoba at Cita con la Vida.

Above: I stopped crying long enough to take a good picture with Alex and Alice.

Right: Alex and Alice share their testimonies with the church.

Last day of the ride with Argentinian rock legend Ulises Eyherabide.

Above:
We made it to the Atlantic Coast!

Right:
Celebrating at the Obelisco in downtown Buenos Aires.

your brain, and has you saying a ton of things you're bound to regret.

"What are you talking about, Adrian? This is so unprofessional."

Adrian's smile evaporated. His face went pale. But I didn't stop. I kept on at him.

"Your number one job is to make sure we have food where and when we need it. It's not exactly difficult and it shouldn't take two hours. Your job's simple, Adrian. And we found our own stale bread without you."

"Don't talk to me that way, Evan. I'm doing everything I can."

"Really?" The anger stepped up a notch. I was yelling now. Practically screaming at him. "Are you sure, Adrian? Because if you are, there's no point in you being here."

It was only when I stopped that I realized everyone was looking at me. The videographers, the other drivers, the riders. Everyone's eyes were on me.

I stepped away and looked at the sandwich that was semi-crushed in my hand. I felt awful, and I knew I'd just been a jerk, but I didn't trust myself to go and apologize straightaway. I was still wired way too tight.

Way to start the ride, Evan. You just showed everyone exactly where your priorities lie: with the program and not the people.

Paul and Pablo both came over to where I was fuming silently.

"Evan," said Paul, his voice quiet but with an unmistakable strength in it. "That is not how you're going to talk to people on this ride."

I looked up. Nodded. I desperately wanted to go back four hours and start all over again.

He smiled. "Eat. Calm down. It's day one. We're gonna get through this. Tomorrow will be better."

I took a bite and tried to let some of the tension go.

"You know, Evan, I think we should call it quits for today. It's okay. We can go back to the house, get some decent food inside us, and start again tomorrow. We can push harder the next few days and make up for what we missed out on today."

* * *

I was seven years old when my family fell apart.

My dad sat me, Lindy, and our brother, Cameron, down and told us that he had been unfaithful to Mom. He said he was sorry. He said it was all his fault and that he was wrong. He was crying as he talked. The tears started flowing even heavier when he asked us to forgive him.

I was too young to understand the subtleties of the conversation. I didn't know what *unfaithful* really meant, and I didn't pick up the different ways that my sister and my brother reacted. I didn't understand that as a pastor, my father hadn't just let down our family but the whole church community as well.

Yet there were some things that my seven-year-old mind did understand: I could tell that whatever *unfaithful* meant, it was a bad thing that caused both my parents a lot of pain. I knew that my dad had broken something precious and that it could not be put back together again, ever. And I knew—the way that I knew the sky is up and the earth is down—that my dad was truly, truly sorry, and that he meant it when he said so.

A while later, when Dad had moved out and

was still banned from attending church, I remember reading about King David. It reminded me so much of Dad: a man who so many people revered, but whose flaws led to his failure. A man who owned up to his adultery and cried out to God for mercy.

The whole episode with my dad wove itself carefully into my own story. I grew up valuing his repentance and his refusal to blame others when he was mistreated himself. I learned to see failure as something that I should first strive to avoid, but that when it inevitably happened, I should repent and ask forgiveness quickly and sincerely.

Even though it put an end to our days as a family of five living under one roof, I'm grateful for the fact that I was always able to keep good relationships with both my parents. Mom has been so steady my whole life, always supporting me, always listening when I need to talk. If my dad has shown me repentance, Mom has modeled what it means to be consistent and unchanging. From Dad I get my spirit of adventure, and from Mom I get the ability to think strategically. I needed to dig deep into both for the ride.

* * *

We were back at Pastor Rodrigo's house by the time it got dark. I took a shower and once I was dressed spent a few moments sitting quietly on my own outside. I could hear the team inside, starting to eat the giant platters of barbecued beef and salad that our host had laid out for us.

It was tempting to stay there all night. It was tempting to go back over all the years I'd known Adrian, trawling for evidence that I could use to justify the anger I had unleashed at the garage. Like so much temptation, there was a part of me that really, really wanted to give in. In spite of all I had learned from my dad's affair, I was struggling to put those lessons into practice.

All I could do was pray. It wasn't eloquent and it wasn't full of victory. It was just a long string of deep aches and mumbled words. "I'm so over my head right now, God. I can't do this on my own."

I found Adrian and apologized. I told him I'd been a jerk and that I was wrong to go off at him like that. I told him that I knew I needed to step up as a leader and that I didn't want anyone on the team to feel the way I'd made him feel. I asked for his forgiveness, and he gave it.

Later, when our bellies were full of salted beef and our eyes were growing heavy, we met as a team.

"Guys," I said. "I was wrong back there. I've apologized to Adrian, and I want to apologize to all of you. I don't want to be that guy who yells like that and who treats people badly. I want to be better."

There were murmurs of people telling me it was okay and smiles of forgiveness. I felt the grace in the room, undeserved as it was.

The meeting flowed from there. We talked honestly and openly about how the ride had gone that day and how we could have done better. It wasn't me leading the conversation, but each person speaking from their own area of expertise. Adrian talked about start times, Paul about the finer points of riding as a peloton. Pablo talked about the importance of having enough food, of keeping in contact with our cell phones, and Essence explained how the support vehicles needed to always be driving behind us, acting as a block between us and traffic.

When it was over, we hugged and laughed and went off to bed, hearts as full as our bellies. I could still feel the embers of shame and regret about how I'd behaved toward Adrian.

I wanted to keep it that way.

* * *

It's a sad truth, but a truth nevertheless: Too often we let ourselves believe that when we're fighting a noble cause, we can justify treating people badly. It's like we think, *If it was okay for Steve Jobs, then it's gotta be okay for me too, right?*

Wrong.

What we do is not more important than how we treat people. In fact, how we treat people and what we do are indivisible. That's true for every one of us, but it's doubly true for Christians—a group who have been specifically, explicitly, and directly ordered to "love your neighbor as yourself" (Mark 12:31). It couldn't be clearer, and yet, still we screw up.

I've seen so many people wounded in churches where some leader has started to believe that the ends justify the means. "It's for the gospel," they say. "We're going to bless people in our work!" While all the time they take advantage of and manipulate those they profess to lead.

Jesus didn't lead like that.

When the people who had agreed to follow Him screwed up, which they did often, He was patient. Kind. Loving. Even when Jesus was stressed to the point of being overwhelmed, He didn't chew Peter out for slicing the guard's ear off in the garden of Gethsemane.

Jesus didn't subscribe to a win-at-all-costs philosophy—at least, not when those costs were going to be shouldered by others. Like many of the best leaders out there, He fixed our mess Himself.

That's what it means to go The Extra Mile.

It means being patient with each other, especially when our resources are low and our stress levels are high.

It means investing in and building up our right-hand men and women, especially when they don't quite reach the standards we set.

It means apologizing when we mess up, but not to try to improve our standing or regain the high ground. We apologize because that's what we're called to do. And requesting the forgiveness of the person we have wronged restores to them some of the power we have taken.

But The Extra Mile isn't just about fixing things when we've blown up and made a fool of ourselves outside a gas station.

Going The Extra Mile looks like the conversation we had as a group. We were tired and full and some of us were definitely feeling kind of raw and wrung out. It would have been so much easier to turn off the lights and go crash out without having that honest, open conversation about how we could improve. It would have been easy to avoid opening up an old wound or introducing new ones, but it would have been a mistake.

Going The Extra Mile means putting people ahead of our goals. It means talking when we'd rather not. It means being patient while we invest in others. It means fixing things that are bent before they become broken. And it means that sometimes, people are going to point out our flaws at the same time that we're thinking of theirs.

I don't want to get to the end of my life and look back and see a trail of damage I've inflicted along the way. I want to look back and see people standing taller, stronger, and happier because of the involvement I've had in their lives.

I guess I want to be a little like Noah… a righteous man. A blameless man. When God told him to make an ark, he obeyed. But all the laughter and mocking and ridicule he received couldn't have been easy to block out. I bet there were moments when he doubted. Had he really heard God right? Was this a leap of faith or a risk that was about to go wrong?

But God chose Noah because he was righteous. He had lived a life that pleased God. But there was something else about him too: He was responsible, rational, creative, logical. He was a distant son of Adam, and he still bore the marks of the true original.

We don't all get the blueprints for our greatest adventure hand-delivered from God. Most of us will stumble along, taking it one day at a time, inching our way along. And that's okay. We don't all have to build an ark. We don't all have to save the world. That's God's job. All we have to do is say yes to what He asks of us.

Chapter Six

Losing Control

Day two was nothing like its predecessor. We said goodbye to our hosts by 9:00 a.m. and had driven to the gas station halfway between Viña del Mar and Santiago by ten. Adrian got food before we began and we set off in a near-perfect peloton with one of the support vehicles acting as our rearguard protection. I felt none of the previous day's stress and frustration, and the whole team seemed to be working as one. Best of all, we encountered precisely zero flat tires. It was as if that first day of *Ciclo Vida* had belonged to another team tackling another ride on a different road altogether.

The highway quickly entered a gentle climb, which in turn became steeper. We got our first glimpse of the mountains that stand sentry around Santiago. Even though I'd seen them plenty of times over recent days, witnessing these epic views from the bike made me appreciate the beauty on a whole new level.

The snatched conversation among us riders turned to what other location it most reminded us of.

"Denver," said Essence and Nathan.

"Geneva," I said.

"Vancouver," said someone else.

Alex said nothing. He just kept on riding. I made a note to think first before starting another conversation where our first world privilege was so clearly on display.

The closer we got to Santiago itself, the stronger Alex became. We passed by wealthy neighborhoods bordered by favelas, and the two-lane highway expanded into a massive five-lane freeway. With every mile, Alex pushed on, cycling harder and faster. By the time we were in the city itself and cycling along the five-mile cycle path that would take us all the way to the end of our day's ride, Alex was in full-on beast mode. With Alice due to start riding with us the next day, it was his opportunity to hold nothing back and show us what he was capable of. If any of us had had any doubts about his abilities as a rider before, those thoughts were now gone.

It took us three hours to ride the forty-six miles that day. As we stood smiling and laughing and celebrating our first milestone outside the presidential palace with coffee, there was a sense that the previous day was truly behind us. Those physical and logistical setbacks that had plagued us on day one were not necessarily going to be permanent features for the rest of the ride. We could ride on with confidence, knowing that together we had what was required to make it all the way to Buenos Aires. It was the same with the relationships as well. I didn't need to worry whether people were holding on to resentment or unforgiveness. They'd told me everything was okay, so it was up to me to believe them.

Sometimes The Extra Mile means changing the way you look at things. It means choosing to trust rather than giving in to doubt.

* * *

The next day there was no riding to be done, just a concert to prepare for. The band arrived—bringing with them my spare bike for Alice—and we spent the day doing all the usual things that have to be done at the start of a tour: some last-minute rehearsing as we ran through the set list, a long sound check, and several hours of just hanging around. It was strange to switch completely out of ride mode and back to music, but I appreciated the similarities between the riders and the band. Both groups understood the importance of teamwork, but also the value of letting each other shine. And when it came to seeing *Ciclo Vida* succeed, they were all willing to put up with some discomfort while in pursuit of the bigger picture.

That night's concert in Santiago was our first chance to see whether *Ciclo Vida* was going to work in the way we hoped it would, leaving people inspired and encouraged to keep going The Extra Mile.

The venue was packed with three thousand people, and it felt right to go all out from the start. I sang a new song that I'd written recently, "La Milla Extra." It's a fun song, the kind that starts out with a clear ascent ahead of it and a distinct message driving throughout.

Everyone thinks I'm crazy
a fanatic radical
A Jesus Freak of nature
Maybe I'm atypical
But I've seen through eyes of compassion
A different of point view
Love that stormed the gates of hell for me and you

When you're onstage you're aware of the way the crowd's mood and focus shift like an ocean in front of you. Sometimes it rushes in, eager to take more of what you've got for them. Sometimes you can feel it start to drain away as the connection between you weakens. Typically, these changes are gradual, shifting slowly verse by verse, chorus by chorus. But there are times when something happens onstage that impacts the crowd so powerfully and so quickly that the shift is almost instantaneous.

That's what happened when I told the crowd that I wanted them to meet two friends of mine from Venezuela and invited Alice and Alex to come on up.

From the moment they stepped onstage—Alice on crutches, the right leg of her jeans knotted and trailing in the space beneath her, Alex with his heavy steel prosthetic catching the lights—it felt to me as though six thousand eyes opened wider. Knowing they were from a failing country whose people were fleeing by the millions, and seeing their disabilities so clearly displayed, the crowd leaned in. The silence was almost total.

"Alice, Alex," I said, bringing them right to the front of the stage. "You know what adversity means. Would you tell us what you know about how an obstacle can be overcome?"

We hadn't planned anything, other than that Alice would speak first and share her story, while Alex would follow. So, once I'd asked my question, I simply handed Alice the mic and stepped back.

She didn't warm them up and she didn't give a whole load of background or context. She didn't need to, because as she juggled the mic with her crutches and shuffled one half pace closer to the crowd, they were ready to soak up every word she uttered.

"One day a few years ago, I woke up in a hospital bed. Somehow I knew that I'd been in there for a while—at least a few hours, and maybe even a whole day. I'd never seen the room before, but I looked around and saw that my mother was there. She was staring at me. She was crying and smiling at the same time.

"There was another woman in the room, a woman I'd never seen before. She wasn't crying or smiling, but instead she was leaning over me from the side of my bed, looking me deep in the eyes. I guessed she was some kind of doctor, because she had a name tag on her blouse and a clipboard down by her side.

"She told me that she wanted to ask me a question and that it was very important. My mouth felt dry, so I just nodded back at her.

"'Alice,' she said. 'What is the one thing that you are most afraid to lose in your life?'

"I knew the answer right away. I didn't have to take a moment to think about it, despite the stranger telling me I could have all the time I needed. But it was difficult to talk because my mouth was dry.

"I told her, 'I'm most afraid of losing someone in my family or not being able to dance again.'

"The woman turned and stared at my mom.

'You haven't said anything to her yet, have you?' My mom shook her head. The tears were still there but the smile was gone.

"The woman moved closer to me. 'Alice, one month ago you were on a motorcycle with your brother. You had an accident and have been here ever since. We had to amputate your right leg. Your brother died in the accident.'

"All I could think of was my brother. I yelled at her, 'Why didn't you want to save my brother's life? Why did you let him die?' She said nothing. Soon I was asleep again. They sedated me for a few more hours."

Alice paused and glanced at Alex. I assumed that he'd heard her tell the story dozens of times before, but it hit me that in a country like Venezuela, where everything was falling apart, these kinds of opportunities didn't really exist. How many concerts were taking place in a country where most people lived in extreme poverty?

"My story did not end there," said Alice, "and I want to tell you that God is capable of giving you second chances."

There was a shift in the crowd as the intensity increased.

"I wanted to be a lawyer, but when I lost my leg I knew that I could not afford to put myself through school. Still, I didn't give up. I refused to give up, because I knew that there was hope for me. I knew that I could continue. I just needed to find a way to do that. And I found it. One day someone gave me a bike to ride, and that was it. I had something to live and fight for. Something that was good in my life again.

"So this is what I want to tell you. I lost my leg and you will lose things too. Some of you have suffered already. Some will face it in the future. But I want to encourage you that if I can overcome obstacles, you can too. If I can find hope, it's there for you as well."

Alice's five-minute talk unlocked something in people. So many of the younger generation in Latin America feel stunted, as if there's a glass ceiling that blocks their progress. They can feel as though there are opportunities on offer to others in the US and Europe, but those same opportunities are simply not available to them. They can feel let down, hopeless. They can feel like they've got nothing ahead of them.

Being a Christian artist, I talk and sing a lot about hope. I tell people that they can find it in Jesus. I believe that with every part of me, but I know, too, that sometimes it's hard to understand. When you feel as if you're missing out on so much that's practical—whether it's money, a job, safety, or a home—then Jesus can seem a long way off.

So, to listen to Alice talk about how she had found hope through something tangible like cycling, it made people listen. And I knew that she was talking about Jesus. She and I had not talked deeply about faith before, but I knew that God was at work in her life. I knew it without a shadow of doubt.

The concert continued to flow from there. Alex spoke a little, sharing some of his own story and explaining how God had restored what he had thought was lost forever. We sang together, three thousand-voices strong, about wanting God to keep us from our comfort zones. We waited and we listened, and we asked God to heal and to lead us. It was a concert in a church with cyclists talking about pain and loss. It couldn't be easily defined, and God breathed life into it.

At the end there was a line of people wanting to talk to Alice and Alex. Everyone I spoke to was amazed by them and wanted to know where I'd found them. I told all of them the truth—Instagram—but I could tell that not everyone believed me.

* * *

The next day we were back on the bikes, but this time things looked a little different. Alice was finally able to ride with us, so our peloton was now seven strong. And the three Nissan trucks that we had been loaned by a generous supporter who happened to be a car dealer were now fully wrapped and emblazoned with the *Ciclo Vida* logo and message. We had Adrian to thank for that, and it was great to see him take pride in having pulled off such a great job. The gas station with stale sandwiches now felt like the distant past.

We were buzzing at breakfast, boosted by the concert and excited by the fact that our next two days on the bikes would take us all the way up into the Andes. The only cloud was the fact that Alice and Alex were not properly equipped for the potential conditions ahead.

August is winter in Chile, and my Google searches had told me that we could expect temperatures as low as fourteen degrees Fahrenheit. There's a thing that can happen to the body when it's being put under extreme physical pressure at high altitude when the temperatures are low. There's a danger that the air an athlete inhales will crystalize in the lungs, leading to potentially fatal blood clots. I hadn't been able to find out much about the condition itself, or the likelihood of one of us falling prey to it, but I wasn't in the mood to take chances. We visited a bike store and fitted Alice and Alex out with full sets of winter clothing, and fingered gloves for everyone else.

We rode sixty miles that day, and it was nothing like the other two days. Having Alice with us, keeping pace with the rest of us, tucking in perfectly to her slot within the peloton, it changed the way the ride felt. It had been great riding with Alex alone, but there was something inspiring about the fact that she had so much more to overcome than he did. He had two sets of quads and hamstrings to drive his pedals round; Alice had only one. She's tiny too, but she rode like gravity and friction and all the other forces of nature had less of a hold on her.

We had left Santiago behind midmorning and had spent much of the day riding through familiar-looking farmland. Forty miles in, though, it changed. The highway started climbing and we passed through a series of towns that looked like they had been settled by German immigrants. It was all beautiful rolling hills and up ahead we could see the Andes.

Alice was slowing a little, but we were doing just fine. Until we heard the police siren behind us.

A cop car overtook us and pulled over ahead. Two officers stepped out and made it clear that they wanted to talk to us.

"You can't ride here," said one.

"No cycling on the highway," said the other.

I was confused. "You're sure? We've been cycling along this highway since Santiago. And we were on the highway from Viña del Mar too. Nobody else has told us we can't."

Both officers stood firm, repeating what they'd said.

"So where should we cycle then? We're staying in the town up ahead. Is there another road that will take us there?"

"No. But you can't cycle here."

We were at an impasse. They decided to check our passports, which took a while to organize. They couldn't find anything to complain about there, so they just went back to their original line.

"No cycling on the highway," said one officer.

"You can't carry on," said the other.

They finally left and we shuffled about for a few minutes, checking maps and confirming that we were on the only road that led to our destination.

"What do we do?" asked Paul.

It seemed simple to me. "We keep riding."

When I decided to start traveling in Latin America, I had a lot of people at my church tell me what they thought of my plans.

"You're going to get kidnapped or robbed!"

"They hate Americans and they'll hate you!"

"It's dangerous down there. You don't know what you're getting involved in."

I've never been kidnapped or robbed. In all the time I've been traveling in Latin America, I've never met anyone who hates me just because of my passport. I've not encountered any kind of danger that made me any more scared than I've felt at home in the US. But they were right about me not knowing what I was getting involved in.

Sometimes ignorance can be a strength. Sometimes going The Extra Mile means taking a big old risk and trusting that God's in control.

Which, when you think about it, isn't a risk at all.

* * *

Nothing could have prepared me for the beauty that was waiting for us the next day. No video could re-create it and no photo could even begin to capture the size and power of the Andes. As we climbed from six thousand feet all the way up to fourteen thousand feet, each switchback opened up some new, dramatic view. If my lungs hadn't already been bursting, the landscape we were passing through would have taken my breath away.

I had woken up nervous that day. The way I saw it, the hardest sections of *Ciclo Vida* were all on the front end of the ride with the ascent from Viña del Mar that would lead us up to the top of the Andes before ultimately crossing over into Argentina. And of the four days we were spending on the ride in Chile, this final one was going to be the toughest of all. Climbing eight thousand feet in one day was a challenge on par with some of the stages of the Tour de France, so I was really worried that the gap in class between me and the other riders was going to show. In the corner of my mind was an image of me struggling at the back of the peloton, broken by the ride and holding the rest of the riders back.

Within an hour of leaving our hotel in the town of Los Andes, those nerves were starting to ease. The ascent was brutal and long. It was too much for Alice, who ended up loading her bike into the vehicle and sitting out the climb. Somehow I was able to keep pace with the other six. I wasn't pushing to be at the front of the peloton, and I was unable to speak, but at least I wasn't getting left behind.

But it was the views rather than the relief that soothed my nerves and calmed my soul. With each switchback there was something new to marvel at: sharp ravines falling away to the side, new views of mountains towering above, epic views that reached farther and farther away. I could only ever glimpse these sights, snatching the briefest of looks here and there before I turned my focus back to maintaining the three-inch gap between me and the rider in front. But even when I wasn't stealing a glance, I could feel the landscape around me. Giants were watching me, looking down as I crawled slowly across the floor.

In those moments, when my lungs and legs were begging me to stop but everything around me was calling me to press on and keep going, I was truly losing myself in nature. I was dwarfed by the world God had created, and it wasn't just okay—it was exactly the way it was supposed to be.

The higher we got, the more snow and ski chalets

we saw, but it wasn't all picture-postcard stuff. We were sharing the road with every other vehicle that was heading from Santiago into Argentina, which meant there were times when our little peloton had to share the road with 18-wheelers. There were too many moments when I genuinely feared that we were going to be crushed.

But if the traffic was worse than anticipated, the weather was nowhere near as bad as we'd feared. It was cold enough that we all needed our winter weather gear when we stopped, but at fifty degrees it was almost perfect for riding.

Sometime around 4:00 p.m. that day, after six hours of brutal climbing, we rounded a corner and felt the road begin to level out. The traffic started to bunch up ahead of us as we finally reached the border with Argentina. Riding from one side of Chile to the other was our first major milestone on *Ciclo Vida*. We only had another five miles downhill to cover that day on the Chilean side of the border, and it felt significant to have made such good time on such a tough day.

We were kind of pumped—pausing for photos and making sure the video guys captured the moment—but the two Argentinian border guards who pulled us over to one side of the road weren't in the mood to join in our celebrations. They just stared, stone-faced, as we wheeled our bikes up alongside the support vehicles and offered our passports to the younger of the guards. He was a kid, really, and he looked nervous as he carefully studied each page of every passport, all the time glancing up at his boss.

"Hey!" The older guard burst to life and marched over to one of the video guys who was trying to capture some B-roll. "Stop that! No filming! Gimme the camera!"

It took a lot of calm talking and apologies to get him to back down and allow us to keep the camera, but he made sure that the guy deleted all the footage he had recorded that day. It was a blow, especially knowing that we'd been riding through some of the most epic views imaginable. And now all of it was lost, and we were facing a short-term problem as well: The guy had clearly decided that he was going to make sure our border crossing was as slow and awkward as possible.

He started by poking his head into the rear of one of our vehicles. He pointed to a couple of cases and indicated that he wanted to see inside. There was nothing much in them other than the usual equipment a video team might have, but it was all expensive, hi-tech stuff. I could feel myself tensing up.

"Why do you have so much equipment?" he asked.

"We're riding from one coast to the other for charity," I said. "We're filming as we go so that we can raise more money."

The old guy did nothing. No shrug, no smile, no nod of approval. He just pointed to a couple more cases and ordered them to be opened as well. When he was done he prowled around the vehicles, staring like he was sure there was something wrong.

The young guy was still doing a forensic study of our passports when the old guy came over to us riders. We'd been waiting there for more than thirty minutes. The cold was starting to bite.

"Serial numbers," he said, pointing to the bikes. "I need to see the serial number for every bike."

I was about to ask him why but changed my mind. He was looking for some excuse to make our lives miserable, and I had a hunch that disrespect or rudeness would qualify. So, we soaked up another thirty minutes showing him the serial numbers on each frame and waiting while he slowly took note of each one. It was agony to have to wait like that, even though we only had another twenty minutes left to ride. The light was starting to fade and the tension among all of us was starting to build. After hours of riding through majestic scenery, feeling dwarfed by the power of nature, we were stuck fast, being held at the whim of a little man enjoying his power a bit too much.

When both guards had searched everything they could possibly search, they disappeared into their office and left us, stuck. All we could do was keep waiting, watching as the last hour of daylight leaked from the sky.

"We have a problem," said the old guard when he finally emerged again, ninety minutes after we'd arrived at the border. "With the vehicles."

I was sure he was mistaken. They were three

Nissans, lent to us by a kind supporter in Viña del Mar. They were pristine, with hardly any miles on the clock. There was clearly nothing wrong with them.

"They are registered in Chile, but you only have two Chilean drivers among you."

He was right, but I still didn't see what the problem was. After standing still for an hour and a half and seeing our riding time fade away, I was wound up tight. So, I took a breath. Tried to calm myself. "I don't understand. Is that a problem, sir?"

"You cannot bring multiple vehicles in on one license. Only one car per driver, and every car must be driven by someone from the country in which it is registered. It's the law."

I checked with everyone else on the team, and nobody had heard of such a law. It was all nonsense. Even the young guard looked confused. So I gave up on the deep breathing and calm talking and went at it.

"That's not a law. Where does it even say that?"

He shrugged. He clearly had no evidence for this weird law, and it didn't bother him at all. We were playing cards, and he was the house. And the house always wins.

"You can only bring two vehicles into Argentina."

"What are we going to do with the third? We can't leave it here."

Another shrug. Not his problem.

"So," he said as he stared at us. "Which vehicle are you leaving?"

Two hours after arriving at the border, we were finally waved through. It had taken at least another thirty minutes to unload the equipment from the least packed vehicle and spread the contents among the remaining two. By the time we were given permission to set off again, the temperature was plummeting, and the light was gone. Ahead of us lay Argentina, bathed in silent darkness.

The good news was that the traffic was gone and we had the road ahead to ourselves. The bad news was that not one of us had brought any lights with us. All we had was individual GoPros on some of the bikes, which only threw out a small pool of light.

"So, how do we do this?" I asked the others as we cleared the border and paused to consider our options.

There was nothing to discuss. There were no good options. All we could do was pull out into the darkness and hope that we'd make it down the mountain in one piece.

What we did was very dumb. But it was fun.

We set off with the vehicles behind us, both with their brights on. They did an okay job of lighting up our path, but they were powerless to pierce the vast darkness that extended beyond the edge of the road. It was like having a wind-up flashlight in the middle of a forest at night: The light made the darkness seem darker.

Instead of riding as a peloton, we kept at least a few feet between us. Paul was in the lead, yelling a steady commentary of what was ahead.

"Debris on left!"

"Watch the corner!"

We were flying. The adrenaline was about as high as I'd ever experienced. I was a kid again, riding wild and free with zero regard for the danger.

How did I get here? How did I end up riding in the darkness down a mountain with no safety rails at the side and nothing but dark, echoing blackness beyond? One slip, one corner misjudged, and any one of us would be hurtling over into whatever cavernous ravine was waiting to swallow us. Death had never been this close. I was nervous and far out of my comfort zone, but thrilled and alive at the same time.

There's a common saying in Mexico that applies to situations like this: When you're faced with a problem that seems impossible to fix and you somehow find a solution, it's called *mexicanada*, or *doing a Mexican*. There's an equivalent in Argentina too—*argentiniada*—but the closest thing we have in the US is probably *doing a MacGyver*.

Back home in the US, we play it safe. There's a lot of good about that, and a lot of pain and suffering gets avoided because of our safety codes. But sometimes that safety-first mentality makes us risk-averse and timid. We miss out on the good stuff and never really find out just what we're capable of.

We covered those five miles in fifteen minutes, not twenty. We arrived at the hotel feeling invincible. All the stress of the border crossing was momentarily flushed from our systems. We'd done an *argentiniada*, and it felt great.

* * *

When it comes to life's challenges, some are like mountains that we can see from a long way off. But not every challenge or setback we meet in life will be visible, predictable, or the kind of thing we can make a plan for. Some will come out of nowhere. Some will be unfair. Some will be cruel and unjustified. Some will leave us feeling hurt or angry; some will make us want to allocate blame or dive into self-pity. There are better ways to respond.

One of the heroes of the Bible is Moses. He's the one who helped rescue an entire nation from slavery, so he knew all about giant challenges and unexpected obstacles. Breaking the Israelites free from Egypt was a colossal challenge, the kind of impossible task that nobody had been able to accomplish before. It must have occupied so many of his thoughts from the moment God challenged him in front of the burning bush right up to the day when Pharaoh finally agreed to let them go. Moses gave us a great model to follow when life throws unexpected problems at us. He planned well for the challenge he could see, making sure the people were prepared for the exodus, giving careful instructions for what they should take with them on the journey. But then, just as they probably believed they were finally free, an unexpected problem arose. Pharaoh changed his mind and set out to recapture his slaves.

Some of the Israelites panicked. Fear enveloped them like fog. But not Moses. He didn't stress or panic or see this unexpected problem as a sign that God's original plan had failed. Why? Because he held on to the words that God had spoken to him right at the start, when Moses stood in front of the burning bush: "I will be with you" (Exodus 3:12).

Those five words were enough. They changed Moses from a privileged, timid prince who ran away to save his own skin into a bold, selfless leader. Those words became the foundation of a confidence that allowed Moses to face down an army. Knowing, remembering, and believing those five words allowed him to stand on the banks of the Red Sea while certain death charged toward them from behind. Holding on to the promise allowed Moses to trust that God was still in charge, still leading His people to freedom.

Our reaction to life's obstacles and challenges—the predictable and the unpredictable alike—can be the same *if* we have a clear sense of purpose in the first place. If we know that we're aligned with what God's called us to do, we can dig in. If we know that we're where He's called us to be, then we can stand firm. If we know deep down that God is with us, then whatever we're facing will be seen in context.

"I will be with you…"

The words weren't just for Moses. They can be for us too. We need them most when we're going The Extra Mile.

Chapter Seven

The Crash

Everyone else was busy eating breakfast, but Alex was sitting still. He stared at the phone I'd just given him, then looked at me and frowned.

"Why?" It was the second time he'd asked me the question, and I went ahead and repeated myself.

"Because you don't have one and this one a spare. As a team, we'd like to give it to you. It's a good phone, and you'll like it way better than your old Nokia. You can use it to listen to music on the ride, take pictures, and have video calls with your family back home."

Alex's eyes went back to the phone. He stared at it for a moment, and I wondered whether he was figuring out how to turn it on. But then something changed. He looked up, grinned, and held the phone up above him like this was the Academy Awards and he'd just won his first Oscar. "Wow! I never thought I'd have an iPhone. Never! And look at this! Thank you. It's amazing!"

He was jumping around for a while, then paused.

"Why...?" he said again, searching for the right words, as if he were trying to unpick a knot that was tied tight. "Why did you invite us on the ride?"

"I found Alice on Instagram and I loved her story. I felt the same as soon as I heard yours too."

"But why are you doing all this for us?"

I finally got it. "I think that God has a bigger plan for you, Alex. I think there's a bigger purpose for you being here. And I think that this phone is just a little token of God's love for you. God wants good things for you, and He will provide for you. He's got a purpose and a plan for your life, Alex. That's the very reason Jesus came to earth—because God is a good Father who loves you."

Alex was crying. It took a while before he could speak. When he did, it was my turn to cry. "My dad left when I was three years old. He has seventeen kids with multiple women. He's never given me anything, and nobody has ever given me anything like this."

That phone was old. It worked fine, but it was old and practically worthless. And yet, as a gift to Alex, its value was immense. In God's hands an everyday item that we could have easily overlooked became a tool that helped open Alex up to a deeper understanding of God's love.

This is exactly in character for how God works, and we shouldn't be surprised by it. After all, if you look in the Bible at Matthew 14, you'll read about one of Jesus' most incredible miracles. He took two fish and five small loaves of bread and transformed them into enough to feed five thousand people. It's a perfect reminder of the way God provides for us.

Being committed to going The Extra Mile means that we try to listen for the moments when God's Spirit stirs us to act. At times, that nudge He gives us might seem like a small thing to us; other times it'll be bigger. Our job is not to filter those nudges out or only step up for the big plays. Our job is to listen and obey, to be God's hands and feet. God can take care of the rest.

* * *

We set out that morning and were soon flying downhill. Alice and Alex were attacking the descent like pros, hunching down to minimize drag, slicing through the corners at the perfect angle and generally showing no sign of nerves at all. I was holding on to my handlebars for all I was worth. According to my GPS, we were reaching forty miles per hour on some stretches, and every moment was a reminder that one small mistake could have serious consequences. Between the switchbacks, the dead-drop ravines, and the less-than-perfect road surface, it was kind of terrifying. A whole lot easier than the previous day's efforts to get uphill, but terrifying all the same.

After an hour, the gradient eased a little, and I was finally able to enjoy the ride. We were surrounded by beautiful rolling hills that made me think of Wyoming, and I felt like there was nothing the ride could throw at us that we couldn't overcome. As the road became flat and we resumed riding in the peloton, we were invincible. Our speed on the flat was a solid twenty-two miles per hour, and even though I was pushing myself to the limit of what was physically possible for me and was struggling to keep up, it was a stellar day of riding. So, when we reached the distance we'd planned on covering and saw that there was still plenty of light left in the day, we pressed on.

We were buzzing when we finally called time on that day's ride. We'd covered seventy miles in three hours, descended more than eight thousand feet, and had not had so much as a flat tire. We were crushing it. From here on, I was convinced that we were going to be cruising along without any stresses at all.

* * *

I had a fever that night. While the rest of the team stepped out into the darkness and marveled at the sight of the Milky Way spread out above them, I was curled up in the fetal position in my narrow hotel bed, hoping that whatever was wrong with me was only temporary.

The next day I was better. Not perfect, but good enough to get on the bike and ride. Only, instead of skipping across the gently rolling hills at the same steady pace we'd been able to sustain the day before, in the morning we were struggling to hit half the speed.

It wasn't anything to do with illness. It was the wind. The day before, conditions had been perfect. Today, we were in the grip of a vicious crosswind that gnawed at us constantly. I'd never experienced anything like it.

Now that we'd cleared the Andes, our aim was to maintain a steady twenty-miles-per-hour pace all the way to Buenos Aires. We'd managed that just fine the day before, but with this new wind constantly attacking us on the right, we were going as slow as nine miles per hour. With eighty miles planned for the day, it didn't take a genius to work out that we were likely going to end up riding in the dark once again. We'd gotten away with it once, but I did not like the idea of trying it again. Besides, battling the wind was draining. If we were going to have to keep up this kind of effort for ten hours, it was bound to have an effect on our performance the following days.

The wind's direction was unpredictable, and the road twisted and turned from time to time. Whichever direction it was coming from was a problem. When the wind was at our side, each gust tried to force us into the middle of the road and into the path of any 18-wheeler that might be passing us at the time. When it was raging full in our faces, the cycling was even harder and dragging our speed down even farther. Worst of all, it never seemed to be at our backs.

Everyone was struggling with the wind, especially Alice. She was a pro, but she was a sprinter rather than an endurance athlete. All her training and all her competitions took place in velodromes, where wind never featured and the races were measured in minutes, not hours. Yet despite being in a totally unfamiliar environment, she was determined and gutsy and unwilling to give up. She'd press on at the back of the peloton, the agony written all over her face.

We'd been at it a couple of hours when we hit a hill, about thirty miles short of the city of Mendoza, our destination for the day. The incline wasn't steep, but with the wind hitting us almost head-on, any upward gradient presented a problem. For Alice, it was too much. She needed help, and so Nathan, Paul, and Pablo took turns riding alongside her, one hand on her back, giving her a little extra momentum. They'd tried it back on the ascent in Chile, and it worked okay. Everyone agreed that I shouldn't try to help out myself, due to the fact that every time I turn around while I'm cycling, I always end up steering off to the side.

The three guys were taking turns pushing Alice along, each one riding alongside her for a few minutes at a time. We were still riding in a loose peloton, but nobody was trying to keep a three-inch gap between themselves and the rider in front. With the wind this unpredictable, we needed to keep our distance.

I was at the back, a little ways in front of the only vehicle that had stayed with us, carrying the video guys and essentials for the bikes. Nathan was out in front. Essence, Alex, and Pablo rode behind him. Then came Paul, riding one-handed beside Alice. There was less than a foot between them, and for the first time that day, we were going along at an okay pace.

For the briefest moment the wind died down.

For a second or two there was nothing trying to force us into the road. But it wasn't permanent. It was a boxer's feint, a move designed to catch an opponent off guard. And like a fighter looking for a knockout blow, it came roaring back. This time, the gust was stronger than ever.

I saw Alice's whole body twitch under the force of the wind. Somehow she kept her balance, but her front wheel twitched and her handlebars jerked over and touched Paul's.

Their front wheels collided, then locked up and came to a dead stop. We were going twenty-one miles per hour, so all that energy and motion couldn't just vanish. It had to go somewhere. I watched as both of their back wheels flipped up, sending them six or seven feet up into the air. For a moment, they were flying. Then gravity took over.

I swerved out of the way and yanked my feet free from my pedals. Then I turned and ran back toward them.

Alice and Paul were both lying on their sides, motionless. It looked like they'd just gotten tired and lain down to sleep.

"Alice!" I shouted. "Paul!"

The others had all stopped. Pablo was waving at traffic, warning them to go around us. Essence and Nathan were standing over Paul. I remember feeling especially grateful that Nathan was with us, him being a med student and all. The video guys had stopped and were running over toward the pileup of bodies and bikes. Alex was with Alice, leaning over her, saying something that I couldn't make out, repeating it over and over. He was kissing her cheeks.

I tried my phone to see if I could reach Lindy. There hadn't been room for her in the two vehicles that morning, so while one of the vehicles had stayed with us, she had waited back at the hotel for the second truck to go back and pick her up once they'd dropped us off. I had no idea where she was now or how long it would take her to reach us. And my cell phone had no reception, so there was no way of finding out.

I went to check on Alice first. She was awake, murmuring a little.

"Alice!" I called, crouching down beside her. "Are you okay?"

She didn't move much, but I thought she gave

me a nod.

"Alice? You're okay?"

She groaned again. Then again. The pain appeared to be increasing. "Stay calm, Alice. Let me get you some help."

I looked over to Nathan. He was crouched down, checking Paul's side. Essence was staring at Paul's head. It looked weird to me too, but I couldn't tell why.

"Paul is bleeding!" Essence yelled.

"Don't take off his helmet!" said Nathan. His voice was controlled, but it was taking him real effort to make it that way.

I ran to Paul. He was lying on his side. His shirt was ripped from the top down. Blood, fabric, and flesh were all mingled together.

"Where's he bleeding?" I asked.

Nathan pointed to his head. I leaned in and saw a streak of blood as thick as my thumb. I looked more closely. That's when I understood what was wrong with his head. His helmet was still on him somehow, but it was broken and bent out of shape like it had been run over by an 18-wheeler.

I'd been feeling the surge of adrenaline ever

since the crash, but now it jumped to something else. Pure fear.

"Hey, Paul!" Nathan said, his voice still strained. "Paul? Can you hear us?"

An engine roar filled my head as a truck crawled past us. Paul was lying there. Not moving.

I started to really freak out now. I thought Paul was dead. I couldn't take my eyes off his helmet. He must have landed right on it—all 230 pounds of him. How could anyone survive a collision that great?

I started crying.

Had I just killed my best friend by inviting him on this ride? What was I going to say to his mom? How could I ever explain any of this? Who the heck did I think I was to bring all these people out and ride these highways with all their danger? Why not just do a normal tour in the safety of a bus?

I felt like breaking down inside.

"Hey, Paul?" Nathan's voice was different. Paul was stirring. "Paul? Hey, buddy. That's right. Stay awake for me now."

Over the next few minutes, as Nathan checked him out carefully, Paul slowly came back around.

When Nathan was done, Paul pushed himself up to sitting. I couldn't believe it.

"You're okay?" I asked, crouching in front of him as Nathan went to check on Alice.

"What happened?" Paul asked.

"Oh man! The wind must have caught you and Alice because you locked up and went flying. Looks like you landed on your head."

"Yeah." Paul nodded, his eyes locked on some point in the middle distance. "So what happened?"

"You fell, Paul. Are you okay?"

He nodded again. Looked at me. His eyes were vacant. The blood was running down his face.

"What happened?"

I forced a smile to try to mask the fear. "Hey, buddy. It's going to be okay."

We sat like that for several minutes. Nathan was trying to encourage Alex to give Alice some space, but it was a constant battle. Alex was crying hard, and all he wanted to do was hold Alice.

Eventually, Nathan sat back.

"I think they're okay to be moved," he said. "But they need to get to a hospital."

My worst fears started to subside, but only slightly. All the time we'd been sitting there, Paul had been asking me the same question—*What happened?*—over and over. I was starting to worry about brain damage. And when Alice got to her feet, she started complaining of a serious pain in her hip. Besides that, they both had some serious cuts that I was sure would require stitches.

I checked my phone again. Still no cell service. We had no way of knowing when the other vehicle would be passing by with Lindy on board, so the only option was to clear our one vehicle of its camera equipment and take Alice and Paul ourselves to the nearest hospital in Mendoza, thirty miles away.

Ten minutes later, Nathan and Adrian drove off with Alice and Paul. The rest of us stood at the side of the road and prepared to wait as long as it took until Lindy and the other vehicle came by. There were all our bikes, bags, and boxes of camera equipment piled around us, at least $10,000 worth. I knew we looked out of place and were likely to attract attention, but for the moment, I didn't care. I was too busy with my own thoughts.

I was lost in a similar kind of feeling as I sat beside the road that day. My mind wandered to what might happen when they reached the hospital. Would they find evidence of internal bleeding? Was Paul's memory loss and confusion an indicator of brain damage? What if they could never ride again?

No bike ride was worth risking that kind of outcome. No fundraiser that wanted to improve people's lives could be a success if the very people doing the ride and raising the money ended up having their own lives messed up in the process.

"Evan?"

I looked up to see Alex standing above me. He wasn't crying anymore, but his eyes were red and raw. He was holding the phone we'd given him the day before. "I can't get through to her."

"Me neither. There's no service out here."

Alex sat down beside me. The tears started again. "I was so freaked out back there. I thought she was dead. I thought I'd lost her."

Everything I could think of saying sounded dumb in my head, so we sat in silence for a while, and I let myself think about Alice and Alex. It was a welcome distraction from thinking about all those possible scenarios that could be playing out at the hospital.

When Alice had first asked if she could bring Alex on the ride, she'd called him her *cycling partner*, and I'd assumed that was exactly what he was—a guy she trained with, nothing more. As soon as I met them at the airport, it was obvious that there was more to their relationship than cycling. They had a way of interacting that went beyond all that. Alex was protective of her, always making sure that she was okay, and when he wasn't close by, Alice would often look for him. At first I didn't necessarily think it was a romantic relationship, but after the crash there was no doubt in my mind. Alex was devastated at the prospect of anything bad happening to Alice. He needed her as much as she needed him. In some ways it didn't change anything at all about the ride, but a part of me knew that if Alice had been injured in a way that made her already-complicated life even more challenging, it was going to affect Alex just as much.

Could a bike ride really be worth that kind of risk?

It was about midday and the sun was hitting us full-on. It was getting kind of warm, and we were trying to find shade beneath our jackets. I started to wonder whether we might have an issue with water.

The sound of a truck approaching made me look up. I hoped it was Lindy, but instead of a brand-new Nissan wrapped in the *Ciclo Vida* logo, it was the *policía*. It stopped beside us and an officer stepped out, wanting to know what was going on.

We explained about the ride and the crash and how Alice and Paul were on their way to the hospital while we were waiting for our other vehicle to come along. I was about to ask whether the police officer had a working cell phone, but he cut me off.

"These friends of yours. What are their passport numbers?"

"I don't know their passport numbers," I said, trying to keep the frustration out of my voice as I tried to think clearly in Spanish. "They have their passports with them, though."

"What about your numbers? I need to see them."

I wanted to ask how that would help anyone but kept quiet and got everyone to do as we'd been asked.

When he was done, the officer turned and started walking back toward his truck.

"Hey," I called, surprised that it was over so quickly. "Can you give us a ride to Mendoza? That way we can get off the road and check on our friends."

He frowned. "No. I can't."

"But the whole bed of your truck is empty. You could fit all our stuff in easily. It's only thirty miles away."

"Mendoza is outside of my jurisdiction. I could take you ten miles, no more."

We traded a few looks among us, then said polite thank-yous and loaded everything into the back and were moved to another part of the road ten miles closer to Mendoza.

It was frustrating to be back waiting, but at least we now had cell service. Nathan was my first call. "Any news?"

"Not yet. We just arrived and they're waiting to be seen." I thought maybe I detected a change in his voice, but I couldn't be sure.

I was just calling Lindy when the other Nissan truck came into view, with her inside.

"You heard about the crash?" I said as she paused at the side of the road while the rest of the team loaded everything but the bikes into the back.

"Yeah. We're going now. Are you okay?"

"Sure."

She sped off, leaving Pablo, Essence, Alex, and me to climb back on our bikes and set off in pursuit.

It was brutal. Partly because we'd stopped, partly because the wind was still attacking us, but the main reason those last twenty miles were so difficult was because right then, being on a bike was the last place I wanted to be. It felt slow and awkward and risky and just plain annoying. All I wanted was to be in Mendoza doing anything I could to make sure that Alice and Paul were okay.

Of course, there was nothing I could do. Nothing other than keep my head down and keep on cycling.

As soon as we reached the hotel, it was back to waiting.

I showered and then spent hours pacing. It was torture, and the only thing that made it bearable was the fact that the others were there too. We could focus our efforts on making sure Alex was okay.

It was dark outside when I received a message from Lindy saying they were about to leave the hospital. I hit reply straight away.

Who? All of you?

Everyone, she replied. *A & P being discharged now.*

The relief was as sweet as any I'd ever felt.

Paul still looked a little shaky on his feet when he walked into the hotel, but his grin told me that everything was all right. He talked us through his injuries—including twenty stitches in the three-inch gash on the back of his head—and we all agreed how lucky he had been.

"I saw the whole thing happen," I said. "I'm really sorry I couldn't warn you to get out of the way."

He looked at me like I was the one concussed. "It's nobody's fault, Evan. It's just one of those things that happens on rides."

I was grateful, but I was also restless. Part of me was desperate to find out what his concussion meant for his involvement in the ride. Was it over, or could he carry on? Selfishly, I hated the idea of him having to quit. Paul didn't just possess the strongest set of quads, glutes, and hammies among us, he was also the real leader of the ride. Maybe it was because he'd completed an epic coast-to-coast ride for charity before, but it seemed to me that Paul was the one who could get people to dig deep and ride hard. When the winds were strong or the gradient steep, it was Paul's voice, not mine, that spurred people on. Losing him for the rest of the ride would damage us.

I was tempted to raise the subject with him, but he was whacked and needed to rest.

I went to check on Alice too. She was just as philosophical about the crash as Paul was.

"If it happens to the pros," she said with a grin, "it'll happen to us!"

I was so impressed. That was not the kind of response I would have had, but Alice was the very definition of tough.

We sat around and chatted for a while. As laughter filled the room, it was almost as if the crash hadn't happened at all. Having spent every hour since the accident feeling regret and remorse about the ride, it was strange to feel my affection for it return. It was only when I was talking to Lindy later on that evening that I found out that the ride wasn't going to be the same.

"They'd just been seen when I got to the hospital," she explained. "I wanted to make sure nothing got missed, so I told them I was a trauma doctor and asked to have a look at the X-rays and CAT scans."

"They were okay with that?"

She smiled. Lindy's not the kind of person to worry too much about things like that. "Paul's scans revealed contusions but nothing more. Alice…"

"What?"

"She'd been telling them that it hurt when she moved and that it didn't feel right. They told her that she was fine and that there was no damage, but the X-rays revealed a clear fracture on her hip."

"You told them this?"

"They took another look and agreed. But at the end of the day, there's not much to do about it other than manage the pain. It's the same side as her amputation, so it's not weight-bearing. It'll heal on its own in time, but she shouldn't ride until then."

"And Paul?"

Lindy shrugged. "We'll see."

I found Alice soon after and asked her how she felt about stopping the ride.

"After everything I've been through, I want to go out and show people what I'm capable of achieving." She shrugged and shook her head. "But for now I have to stop."

Selfishly, I was sad. Alice hadn't been at all comfortable when she'd been a passenger in the vehicle on the first two days of the ride, and so I kind of assumed that she might just want to head back to Chile straightaway. That would mean no more Alice getting up and speaking at the concerts, which sucked.

"Going back to Chile might be the best thing for your hip," I said as we discussed it. "Those guys will take care of you until we finish the ride."

Alice didn't agree. "I want to be here. I want to finish with you guys. Even if I'm not cycling, I'm going to be here supporting you."

I was in awe of her resilience and her strength.

One sore arm and I'd turned my back on wrestling forever. Alice had just been involved in a crash that—if it weren't for those helmets—could have ended up with one fatality, maybe two. She had so much more to lose than anyone else, and yet she was still determined to keep going. She wasn't interested in playing it safe. She was living without restrictions.

I realized that I had been wrong about Paul. He wasn't the only strong rider in the group or the only leader capable of inspiring the others. Alice was probably the most remarkable person I'd ever met.

I'd given the ride two parts to its name: *Ciclo Vida* and *The Extra Mile*, kind of like a title and a subtitle. I'd chosen them both because they sounded like a good fit for what we were hoping to achieve. It was only now that I fully understood what the full title really meant and how Alice epitomized it perfectly: It wasn't about breaking a sweat, raising some money, and then going home. It was a chance to try to live more fully, to push ourselves further in every way, not just out there on the bikes. More courage. More resilience. More trust.

If there's one story from the Bible that resonated with me louder than any other during the ride, it was Nehemiah's. The man who had returned from exile to rebuild the temple walls faced so much opposition, yet he remained focused and determined on the task ahead of him. "I am doing a great work," he said when opponents tried to get him off task (Nehemiah 6:3).

Paul and Alice were just as focused, just as determined, just as convinced that they were engaged in a righteous task. Even though Alice's ride was over, she remained with the team and did all she could to keep us going. Paul missed just one day's riding. They both understood that the journey was bigger than the pain.

* * *

In my business there's a lot of potential for the ego to get out of whack. There have been plenty of times when I've believed a little too much in my own might and power. I like the way I can put a melody together, and I like the moments we create in a concert when thousands of people are sharing the same joy-soaked moment. Humility is a constant challenge, which is why I love the song "The Reason I Sing" by Jimmy Needham. In it, he sings about being just fine with small stages, small crowds, and small pay. Even if we are serving in the small spaces, in smaller, less-seen ways, our obedience still brings God glory.

Ciclo Vida took us to small stages, and we ended up spending way more than we earned, but in it I was reminded of the most powerful truth: God is constantly inviting us to go deeper with Him. Just like Jesus with the disciples and the rich young ruler, He's offering us to experience more of our relationship with Him. He's constantly standing there, arms wide, beckoning us toward Him. And it's when we take those steps in His direction—the ones that take us out of our comfort zone, the ones that propel us to travel The Extra Mile—that we move a little further away from the place where we're tempted to believe that our egos can run the show. Because when we get truly caught up in the work that God's doing, it's clear that trusting Him is the only way to go.

There were so many times on the ride when I looked around me and realized that there was no way on earth that Evan Craft could have pulled something like this off. Even our amazing team couldn't have done it. It was only God.

That's why the second verse of "The Extra Mile" meant so much.

I used to think that I couldn't change anything,
Because what difference does one man's life make?
But He who left the 99 for me,
Doesn't forget the weak and the fragile.
In the days that my strength fails,
I'll look up at the cross
And I'll remember what You did for me
That every drop of blood is an ocean of grace.
[Paraphrased from the Spanish original]

Chapter Eight

Why We're Here

Mendoza was the three-hundred-mile mark on the ride, one-third of the way toward our final destination. We had always planned to pause the ride there and make the city our base for a few days. We had scheduled a concert at a local church there, and we were all grateful for the opportunity to forget about our bikes for forty-eight hours and take time to recover.

For Lindy, though, it wasn't a pause. It was more significant than that. Our first full day in Mendoza marked both her thirtieth birthday and her last day with us on *Ciclo Vida* before she flew home. It was a day for celebrating and saying goodbye, which left me in a reflective mood.

It had been great having her with us for the first part of the ride, and not just because of how she'd been able to help after the crash. Lindy's presence throughout had meant so much to me. Having my big sister there made me feel protected in ways I hadn't anticipated. When I blew up on the first day, she didn't freak out at me. When I was stressed about the mountains, she didn't doubt me. Whenever I felt out of my depth, she was still there, not panicking or doubting what we were doing. Just having her there was enough.

Lindy was due to fly out while we were doing a concert that night, and we said goodbye after the sound check. I wasn't surprised that I started feeling emotional as we hugged, but I wasn't expecting tears from her. Lindy's not the crier in the family. That's my job.

But there we were, at the back of the church saying goodbye, and Lindy's face was a mess of tears.

"I can't believe it," she said.

"What? Being so old?"

She sniffed at my joke. "No. I can't believe how you guys have treated each other. I've never seen people act in such a selfless way. You guys really love each other."

"You noticed that?"

She nodded. "When I get home, I want to find a Christian community. I want to go back to church."

"Really?" Now it was my turn to cry. This was huge.

We hugged again, and then it was time to go. I walked her out to the front where a car was waiting to take her to the airport.

"By the way," she said before she closed the door, "Alex really needs a new prosthetic."

The concert itself was good, though a little odd without either Alice or Paul—who usually played guitar—up there with us. Between their absence and Lindy's exit, the whole thing felt different. But when Alex came up onstage and told his story, I was still blown away by the way he was able to connect with the people.

By the time I got to bed that night, my head was spinning. Between Paul's involvement in the rest of the ride, Lindy's new desire to go back to church, and her comment about Alex needing a new prosthetic, plus a whole bunch of other things like the ride's financial position and how much money we had been able to raise, my thoughts were jumping around from one thing to the next. I was tired and in need of sleep, but sleep wasn't on the menu.

Of all the things that I was thinking about, money was my biggest worry. When I'd first started planning *Ciclo Vida,* I'd had a clear goal: Raise $100,000 and give it away to a local nonprofit that would directly benefit local people. Only one part of that plan remained solid—the nonprofit who was going to receive the money raised. It was based in Mendoza and did great work feeding malnourished kids. I was due to meet with them the next day, which was the cause of so much of my stress that night.

The first part of the plan had failed. When we had booked the tour, we had agreed with each venue how much we would be paid, always working in US dollars. Between that and what I assumed we'd make from merch sales, the $100,000 figure had looked reliable. Then Argentina entered a full-blown monetary crisis. The peso devalued just before we started the ride, dropping overnight from twelve pesos per dollar to forty. And with the country in financial turmoil, no church could afford to pay us almost four times what we had agreed. Some of them could barely afford to pay us at all.

I was wrestling hard with it all. Part of me saw it as something I simply could not control. I had to trust God in it, to remember He was the provider and that this was not about our skill as fundraisers. We were soldiers, not artists. God would handle the money any way He wanted.

But this whole thing was starting to cost a lot of money, so trust wasn't always easy. With the churches unable to pay, I was funding the ride myself. I'd done okay in the past and I had some reserves, but they were draining fast. Soon, there would be nothing left. I didn't want to reach a point where something went wrong and I didn't have the resources to get us out.

I should have trusted God completely, and looking back now, it's easy to see His hand and His provision in it all. But at night, when you're tired, it's not always easy to be the soldier you want to be.

There was one upside to the peso's crash: Our

costs in Argentina were lower. I was particularly grateful for this when it came to the hospital bill. On the afternoon that Paul and Alice were having their X-rays and CT scans, I did some mental calculations about how much it might all cost. I knew about medical bills in Chile and Colombia and figured that if we'd been there, the total bill would have been in the region of $5,000 or $10,000. In the US, without insurance, it would have been three or four times that much. But Argentina? I had no idea. All I knew was that whatever the final bill was, the devaluation of the peso two months earlier meant it would be four times cheaper. I was just praying that it wouldn't bankrupt us.

When Adrian handed me the copy of the invoice, I was shocked. I couldn't take my eyes off it. I ran through each item several times over—CT scans, X-rays, wound dressings—checking and rechecking the sums.

"You're sure about this?" I asked him.

Adrian nodded. And smiled. "I paid it myself," he said. "In cash."

The total bill was $15.

Thank You, Jesus, for Argentina's universal health care.

* * *

With the struggle to reach our fundraising target, I'd put together a GoFundMe page. I'd shared it once or twice, and in the days before I flew down to Chile, the total stood at just over $2,000. Then the email came in.

At first I thought it was a joke.

"Hey, Evan. I've seen the page and love what you're doing. I want to give $10,000 to support the ride. How can I get you the money? Katherine, Brisbane, Australia."

My reply was short: "Ha ha. Evan." I paused before sending it and added a PS with my number. Just in case.

The next day my phone lit up with a call from Brisbane.

"Is that Evan?"

"Yeah."

"This is Katherine."

"Yeah?"

"I emailed you about donating to the ride."

"Oh..." Maybe this wasn't a hoax after all. "I didn't think you'd call."

"Really? I love what you're doing with this ride of yours. I think it's really cool. Send me your bank information and I'll wire the money."

We talked for a while, then hung up. I still wasn't sure if she'd come through, but a couple of days later there it was: $10,000 just like she'd promised.

I called her as soon as I'd checked my bank account and thanked her. I was curious as well and wanted to know more about her.

"Well, I'm not really wealthy, but I did well with some stocks. I've got a question for you too, Evan."

"Fire away."

"Can I come on the ride? I don't want to ride or anything, but I love the idea of coming and hanging out with you, to see what you're doing."

It wasn't a hard question to answer. "Katherine. You're the biggest donor, so you do whatever you want."

Katherine arrived in Mendoza the same night Lindy left. She'd never been to Chile or Argentina before, spoke no Spanish, and didn't know anything about bikes, but she was a perfect addition to the group. As I introduced her to the team, she told them how God had just put it on her heart to give the money away, and that the very next day she'd made the same amount back on another trade. She was a fellow Extra Miler through and through.

I took Katherine with me the next day to meet the nonprofit we'd arranged to give the money to. I was excited to meet them in person for the first time. Even though our original figure of $100,000 had now shrunk to $12,000, I knew that the money still had the potential to do good and change lives.

The meeting was scheduled for ten in the morning, with a half hour for chatting followed by a press conference that they were going to organize. We hoped it would help raise their profile and maybe bring in some last-minute funding.

We showed up on time and were the first ones there. So we waited. We waited ten minutes. Then twenty. When it was getting close for the press conference, we put in a call to the guys from the nonprofit. They didn't answer.

The time for the press conference came and went. Maybe fifteen journalists showed up. But nobody from the nonprofit.

We waited longer; they didn't show. We called, but they didn't answer.

I was tempted to feel awkward with Katherine being there. She'd given a lot of money and I hated that she might think we were incompetent or untrustworthy. But Katherine wasn't so easily thrown off course, and she just shrugged and said, "I guess God's got a better plan for the money. We've just got to figure out what it is."

Eventually, we gave up and went back to the hotel. In a weird way I was kind of relieved by it all. The thought of handing over a check and walking away felt anticlimactic, like it wasn't a good fit with the way the rest of *Ciclo Vida* had gone.

And Katherine was right. The challenge ahead was different now. We just needed to fall in step with God.

A few days later we did hear from the nonprofit. They apologized for not showing up to the meeting and explained their reason: They hadn't believed that we were for real and had assumed we were laundering money or doing something illegal. We explained the truth and they were okay with it. They didn't ask us for the money, though, and I was glad about that. Because by then we had found a much better use for it.

* * *

The next day Paul was feeling better, and even talking about rejoining the ride in a day or two. That gave the rest of us a boost, and we decided to head out and cover some miles so that when Paul was ready he had a little less farther to go.

Our next main destination was Córdoba, 350 miles away. The route was flat and we figured that over a day or two we might be able to cover anything from 100 to 150 miles. We'd take it easy, though, not putting too much pressure on ourselves. We'd ride as far as we could each day, then climb into the vehicles and head back to Mendoza.

That first day was a disaster. I started feeling like I was dehydrated the moment we left Mendoza, and by the time we reached Las Catitas forty-five miles away, I'd gotten so sick that I was struggling to stay on the bike. The others were happy to call it a day, so we loaded up and turned back, hoping for a better day to come. I was sure that all I needed was an early night and plenty of fluids.

My recovery didn't go as planned. I missed the next day's riding, as well as the day after that. All I could manage was to lie on the back seat of the truck, curled up in the fetal position, shivering like a wet dog. Somewhere in the middle of those days, there was a concert too. I was able to dose myself up with painkillers and flu remedy, but even so I could barely sing at all.

By the time I was ready to resume the ride, Paul was back on his bike. He'd put in a day when I'd been curled up in the truck. He was still feeling sore from the crash, but he'd pressed on all the same.

"A lot of people have to live with discomfort," he'd said when I asked him if he was sure he wanted to ride. "Let's keep going."

When I was finally well enough to get back on the bike and rejoin the others, Córdoba was just two hundred miles away. We figured a day, maybe two tops. We didn't count on the weather having its say.

We set off that morning and were immediately pushed back by headwinds reaching twenty-two miles per hour. We should have been cranking along at twenty miles per hour, but instead we were struggling to maintain a steady ten. My watch told me that there were times when I was expending more energy to go eight miles per hour than I had on previous days on the flat when we'd hit twenty.

It was brutal. And then it started raining.

The storm was swirling around us like ocean riptides. The wind was driving the rain into our faces. Then the rain turned to hail.

We tried to make our peloton as tight as possible, but it didn't make as much difference as it usually did. It was the same result when we tried to use one of the vehicles as a windbreak ahead of us. The storm was still able to break through the gaps and send hail to bite and snipe at each one of us. And when we finally stopped, the conditions got even worse. The hail that had been the size of blueberries was suddenly the size of baseballs. I'd never encountered conditions like it.

There were times when I got scared that day. My fingers were so numb they felt like they belonged to someone else entirely. When I tried to change gears, there were moments when I just couldn't get my fingers to move at all. My hands were so cold, and I was having to grip my handlebars so tight to stay upright against the wind, I was scared that I might fall.

I thought about the setbacks and discouragements we'd faced, some of them as invisible as the wind. There was the crash, the nonprofit not showing up, the days I'd lost due to sickness. It was so tempting to be discouraged, especially as we were on what was supposed to be the easy part.

We could have stopped, I guess. But nobody was in the mood to quit. Paul had chosen to pick himself up and ride through the pain, and Alice and Alex had given us the most powerful demonstration of what it means to be resilient in the face of difficulties and setbacks. There was no way we were going to let a little wind and rain stop us.

Instead, we battled. We were all exhausted. All locked in our own worlds, digging deep and finding whatever resources we could to keep pushing on. I can't tell you how the others got through it, but I know how I did.

I had the lyric from "The Extra Mile" on repeat in my mind:

El día en que mis fuerzas fallan
Pensaré en Jesús
Cargando mi pecado,
Llevando mi cruz.

When my strength fails,
I will think of Jesus
Carrying my sin, carrying my cross.

It's easy to fall into the trap of thinking that life should be easier than it is. When life gets tough, it can be so tempting to say, "It wasn't supposed to be this way."

Really?

Are we sure?

Is life supposed to be free from opposition? Are there never meant to be obstacles? Are we supposed to go from cradle to grave without times of feeling like we were being pushed to our limit?

We're wounded souls carried by mortal bodies, living among people who are every bit as fragile and messed up as we are. Of course life is going to be tough at times. We're going to have setbacks and obstacles and bad days and difficult seasons. And the ones that will hit us the hardest are likely to be the ones we don't see coming.

But that's not the whole picture, and it's not the way the story ends.

We don't battle alone. We aren't designed to struggle without help.

"Do not fear," it says in the Bible. Not once or twice, but 365 times.

There will be trouble ahead, difficult days that will push us. We'll find our edges, reach our limits. And though much of this might be frightening, we do not need to let fear have a grip on us. We can think of Jesus. We can look to Him for the strength that we need to keep on going. And we can trust Him to be there for us—in The Extra Mile. That's where we discover what it means to belong to Him.

* * *

After two days of battling the winter winds on the road to Córdoba, we finally got there, though there was little time to rest. The others on the team joined us and we locked our bikes away and all took a flight five hundred miles north to Resistencia for a concert. It was good to see everyone gathered in the airport, laughing and joking with each other as we made our way through security. I loved seeing the way the musicians, riders, and crew interacted as one team, welcoming Katherine and making her feel at home. Lindy's words about the love on display among us rang loud in my mind.

There was just one thing I didn't like to see. After so much riding, Alex's prosthetic was making his leg sore. Alice was still in pain, and I saw through fresh eyes how difficult life was for them. Watching them struggle through security reminded me how much I took for granted. Seeing them do so with such grace, determination, and peace reminded me of how much in awe of them I was.

Somewhere between takeoff and landing, an

idea started to form in my mind. It wasn't much more than a vague sense at first—more of a what-if instead of anything concrete. But the more I thought about it, the bigger it became. Soon it had a life of its own, and by the time we had made it to our hotel in Resistencia, I was ready to put it into words.

"Why don't we use the money we've raised to buy Alice and Alex new prosthetics?"

The first time I said it out loud, it was to myself, alone in my hotel room. I liked the way it sounded, and it made perfect sense: Between Katherine's generosity and the GoFundMe, we'd raised $12,000. The nonprofit in Mendoza was a dead end, and it would take time to find another cause where we could be sure the money would be well used and make a real impact on lives. Alice and Alex were both in need of prosthetics, and if we were able to supply them, there was no doubt in my mind that their lives would be transformed.

It made sense to me, but I had no idea whether it would make sense to anyone else.

So the second time I said it out loud, it was to Katherine.

Her response was immediate. "I love it. And I can give you another $7,000."

There was time to kill that afternoon, and I spent it googling the strange new world of prosthetic limbs. What I discovered left me a little shocked.

I found out that prosthetic limbs are like cars, road bikes, and any other bit of precision engineering: There's almost no end to the level of skill and innovation on offer. At the head of the pack are prosthetic limbs that reminded me of transformers, made of carbon fiber with inbuilt microprocessors that constantly monitor and adjust themselves to support the user. And just like cars and road bikes, the price tag can get real high—hitting six figures for a limb made by the market leader, Ottobock.

Obviously, there was no way we could even get close to that kind of budget, so I carried on looking. I found some brands that were a lot cheaper, but I had no idea whether a cheap prosthesis would be an improvement for Alex or even for Alice. Was our budget so low that the whole idea was a giant mistake? I had no idea. But then I figured that since I knew nothing about any of this, what I really needed was someone who did.

My searching took another Google route, and I started looking for prosthesis suppliers in Argentina. And that's when I hit gold, finding an orthopedic center right there in Córdoba, where, once the concert was over, we were going to be based for the next week.

I reached out to Deborah, a new contact I'd made in Argentina who worked for a multinational corporation. Like Katherine, she'd reached out when she heard about the ride and offered to do whatever she could to help. Since the nonprofit in Mendoza had assumed I was some kind of criminal, I figured that an approach to the orthopedic center was way better coming from Deborah than from me.

"They're so excited," she said, less than an hour after I'd called her and asked her to help.

"Really?" I was doubly shocked.

"Yeah. They would love to meet Alice and Alex. They'll pick them up from the airport when you get back tomorrow, take them to lunch, and see what they can do."

"Wow. That was a lot easier than I'd thought it would be."

Deborah laughed. "The owner's a Christian. He gets what you're doing with *Ciclo Vida* and he loves it."

The call ended and I slumped back onto my bed. I was astounded and excited, convinced that I was seeing the first signs of God at work. I felt a little less excited when it dawned on me that I'd forgotten to ask Deborah about money, but what could I do? If God was in it, money wouldn't be a problem.

* * *

There are times when concerts feel like a battle. You're onstage in front of people and you can see the resistance among them and sense the hesitation. On those nights your job is to press on regardless, to lead by example as you throw yourself into it all. Then there are concerts when everything feels different: The people are hungry for God to do whatever it is that He's going to do. On those nights, your job is simply to get out the way and let things flow.

The night we played in Resistencia, it was one of the most amazing nights ever. The concert was intense in the best way possible. Paul was back playing guitar, Pablo preached, and there was the strongest sense that the people who'd come were open and ready for whatever God had in store for them that night. It wasn't so much a night where I had to lead. It was a night for me to go along for the ride and watch God change lives.

Alice and Alex were there, and I invited them up to speak just like we had before the accident. This time, however, there was something different about the way they spoke. Just like the rest of the room, they sounded like they were more open to God. We'd talked about faith before, and they didn't see themselves as Christians. But as Alice shared her story and talked about what it meant to find hope after her accident, I knew that God was at work in her.

On other nights, after Alice had spoken, Alex said a few words himself. But this time we had a different plan, and instead of handing him the microphone, I gave him my guitar. I stepped back and listened to him sing.

He played the guitar like he was riding his bike up a steep hill, stamping down on the strings as he powered through the chords. His voice was shaking just a little as he began singing in Spanish. The melody high and wavering, unable to hide the pain that lay deep within the lyrics:

I've been looking for a way out of what
I couldn't understand,
What I don't want to accept.
In seconds life surprises you,
Not knowing what is going to happen.
Don't know if I should stop or continue.
It hasn't been easy but I confess that
I met someone special.
He helped me out of this agony.
Even though you can't see Him.
He's always there for me.

Paraphrased from the original Spanish.

It was all so raw and so real.

When he was done, for just a moment, there was perfect silence in the room.

Just like all the other concerts, the evening ended with people wanting to talk about Alice and Alex. Some of them came up to me and asked where I'd found them; others just wanted to tell me how powerful their story was and how much they'd appreciated hearing it. Just like before, Alice and Alex hung around and talked with anyone who approached them. This time there were more people, and I watched as one woman brought her two young daughters up and introduced them.

"See her, kids? She's a superhero. She's a cyclist and she goes anywhere. Nothing stops her."

Alice laughed and tried to brush it off, but it was clear that the compliment went deep. She was glowing.

Later, when we were back at the hotel and people were just about to crash out, I sat with Alice and Alex in a quiet corner.

"I heard that woman call you a superhero," I said.

Alex's smile was a mile wide.

"I have three younger sisters and I want them to see that if I can, they can too," Alice said, her face glowing. "There are no limitations."

"That's right," I said. "Life isn't easy for you both, but you're so resilient. That's what impresses people so much."

I paused, wondering if this was the right time.

"You know, I've been thinking about what we're going to do with the money we've raised. I think the best thing we could possibly do is see if we can use it to buy each of you a new prosthetic leg. What do you think?"

Immediately they both tensed up. It was like I'd just told them that something terrible had happened, like they were being deported back to Venezuela in the morning.

"No," said Alice without hesitating. "I don't want it."

"I don't either," said Alex.

I looked at them both carefully. They weren't jokers, so I guessed they were serious. But I couldn't understand why. "Let me explain," I said. "We want to get each of you a new leg. It would be yours to keep and you wouldn't owe anyone anything for it. It would be a gift. Like the phone. Wouldn't that be good for you? Wouldn't that help?"

They looked at each other for a moment.

"We've been promised this before," said Alice, her voice quiet. "Lots of times. People tell us that we're going to get new legs or be sent to compete internationally, but it never happens. They always find a way of backing out. We don't want to be let down again."

They sat back, holding hands.

I wanted to respect their wishes, and I didn't take what they said lightly. I would have backed off if I thought that the plan was risky or there was a chance that it wouldn't all work out. But I had a hunch—no, I *knew*—that God was at the heart of it all. And God doesn't play games with people.

"This isn't like all those other times," I said. "I really think that God wants to do something wonderful in your lives."

* * *

Our flights back to Córdoba were delayed, so the next day there was a lot of time spent waiting around the hotel and then the airport. I didn't want to pressure Alice and Alex, and I trusted that if God had orchestrated events this far, He didn't need my help to overcome this little hurdle.

So I wasn't surprised when Alice came over to talk to me at lunch.

"If you're really sure about this, Evan, we'll meet with them."

I told her I'd set it up and got back on the phone to Deborah to make the arrangements.

The rest of the day was a blur as we traveled back south. I didn't get to talk to Alice and Alex much on the flight, and as soon as we arrived at the airport, they were greeted by someone from the orthopedic center and taken away. They looked kind of nervous as they left. I felt like a parent at the start of a new school term. And when Alice and Alex came back to the hotel later on that evening, they didn't seem to be in the mood to talk too much about it all. I was desperate to find out what had gone on, but I could understand their reluctance to talk.

It wasn't until the next day, a Tuesday, that I heard from the center. I was standing in the lobby of the hotel when the call came in, and it was hard to hear the man on the other end properly.

"Evan? This is Dr. Mario from the orthopedic center. We had a good time with Alice and Alex yesterday."

"Yeah? You can help them?"

"We can. Alex doesn't need anything too fancy, as his amputation is below the knee, but there are two options for Alice, both made by a company called Ottobock. They're really good prosthetics and it's going to be about $9,000 for him and about $15,000 for her."

I was shocked. Twenty-four thousand dollars for two prosthetic limbs was way cheaper than I'd assumed it would be, especially as Dr. Mario was talking about supplying them with limbs made by the best company out there. But $24,000 was more than our $18,000 budget.

Six grand. I could find that, right? I could ask around and talk to a few people I knew who had money, and one of them would surely cover it. Or we could do something online and make it one of those community things where everybody throws in a few dollars and raises the money that way. But my gut wasn't telling me to do that. Instead, I was thinking back to the book about Reinhard Bonnke and the way that he put himself in a position where he had to trust God. I was thinking about all the stories I'd heard when I was growing up in California, like the one about the Dream Center in LA. They wanted to buy a $30 million dollar hospital and use it for their ministry but didn't have enough money. But they trusted God and had the faith to ask and ended up getting the place for something like $6 million.

I took a breath.

"Dr. Mario? I've got to be honest with you here. We only have $18,000. Is there any way you can give us a discount?"

"Evan, I'm a Christian," he said, not skipping a beat. "I love what you're doing. Let me talk to the brand and let me talk to my boss. I'll get back to you."

The call ended and I looked up. Everyone from the team had gathered around and had been following the call. Now they were looking eagerly at me. I filled them in on what Dr. Mario had said and told them that he'd be calling back.

"When?" asked Essence.

"I don't know. The supplier's in Germany, so it'll take a while, I guess."

Five minutes after I'd finished with Dr. Mario, my phone rang again. It was the same number.

"Weird," I mumbled. "Maybe he forgot to ask something."

"Dr. Mario?"

"Evan. You got it."

"What?"

"We can do both prosthetics for $18,000. You'll have them on Friday."

I didn't just lose it a little bit. I lost it big-time. I was crying, weeping, saying "thank you" over and over. I couldn't believe it. Back when I'd been dreaming about the ride, I'd assumed that we were going to be raising thousands and thousands of dollars, all of which we'd be able to give away to the causes we encountered. But the reality was different. We weren't raising anything like the figures I'd thought we would, and yet somehow we had received exactly what we needed.

It was like the Israelites in the desert when God

provided them with manna to feed them each morning. He didn't give them more than they needed, didn't allow them to store it up for the next day. He gave them just enough, and it kept them dependent on Him.

The call ended and I looked up at the team. They were crying too, just as amazed, just as stunned, just as grateful as I was.

We took a moment to celebrate, then I wiped the tears from my face and called Alex and Alice.

They both appeared.

"Hey," I said. "I just spoke with Dr. Mario. You guys are gonna get brand-new prosthetics. They're gonna fit them for you, and you're gonna have them this week. On Friday. This isn't a joke. It's really happening this time."

At first, the only thing their faces registered was shock. But there was no disbelief, no doubting me this time. God had been at work with them, filling them up on hope, letting them know that He loved them and that He was for them.

So the shock didn't last longer than a few seconds. And when it left, joy flooded in.

Alice squealed. Alex jumped. Both of them

were crying, just like the rest of us crowded around the phone.

"This is just the start," I said when there was a pause in all the shouting that was long enough for me to speak. "God is going to do incredible things in your lives."

Chapter Nine

Shoe Shopping
(and Other Miracles)

The third time we heard the familiar sound of police sirens behind us, I didn't care. We were exhausted, burning over four thousand calories a day, putting in six-hour shifts in an attempt to cover the 240 miles between Córdoba and Rosario in three days, but I wasn't frustrated. The road surface was bumpy and my butt had reached a whole new level of sore, but I didn't care about that either. I didn't feel stressed or frustrated or worried like I had when we'd been stopped those two times in Chile. Nothing could put a dent in my mood. I just pulled over at the side of the road and waited for the police to get out of their vehicle and figure out what on earth they were going to do with us.

It was Thursday, two days after Dr. Mario had given us the news that Alice and Alex would be getting new prosthetics. I was still buzzing. We all were. Even though there was another day to wait until they were fitted with their new prosthetics, I couldn't stop celebrating. It was like that moment when you hit the ball and know that it's going to score. It's still flying through the air, but you know it's a winner. That's how I felt about Alice and Alex. I knew that God had done it, that the win was on the way as sure as the sun would set that night and rise the next day.

On those two days of riding between Córdoba and Rosario, I'd had one particular song on repeat: "Galileu" by the Brazilian artist Fernandinho. My Portuguese isn't great, so I couldn't understand every line, but the song itself was a perfect soundtrack. I'd put my head down and pedal hard, my soul focused on the Galilean I was following. I'd been in tears much of the time, and there were moments when the joy and gratitude within me was so strong I thought I'd burst. The ride as a whole was nothing like I'd planned, but it was the greatest adventure I'd ever been involved in. I didn't even mind that I'd just completed the longest day's ride—104 miles over seven hours. It all paled in comparison to what God was doing.

As soon as we were told to pull over at the side of the road, I could feel the hunger stirring within me. We'd picked up some *alfajores*—chocolate cookies—back in Córdoba and I had two with me in my jacket. Within twenty seconds I'd swallowed both, grateful for the six-hundred-calorie boost I'd just given myself. I'd come a long way from my hangry outburst at Adrian on the first day but didn't want to take any chances.

"You cannot cycle on the highway," said the officer as he strolled over toward us.

"Okay," I said between mouthfuls of water. "We're going to Rosario. What are we supposed to do?"

The officer waved in the direction we were headed. "You can cycle as soon as you get through the next tollway. It's twenty miles from here."

On both those other times when we'd been

stopped by the police, I'd seen them as an obstacle, something that we needed to overcome or work around in some way. It was different now. We'd gotten the prosthetics, and we knew what the real purpose of *Ciclo Vida* was. This was a battle we didn't need to fight. We did what he said and drove the next twenty miles to the tollway, then cycled the final ten miles into Rosario before loading ourselves back into the vehicles and driving the four hours back to Córdoba.

* * *

We were scheduled to play at a large conference in Córdoba on Friday afternoon and Saturday night, so I wasn't able to be with Alice and Alex when they went back to the clinic for their fitting on Friday. But I heard about it, and I've watched the footage that the video guys captured there so many times, it's like I was in the room with them myself.

Both of them were nervous when they arrived and were greeted by Dr. Mario. Alice held back a little and Alex looked kind of tense. I guess after being promised so much over the years and having it taken away, it's difficult not to be hardwired for disappointment.

But it didn't take long for the truth to dawn on them: This was real, this was happening. Nobody was playing games with them.

Dr. Mario's team split into two groups and took Alice and Alex to different sides of the room. There among the parallel bars and crash mats, the mirrored walls and the assorted exercise equipment, Alice and Alex were both presented with their new limbs.

There was no shouting or screaming for joy. It was quiet in there, not somber, but serious and almost reverent. Dr. Mario took care to make sure that each limb was fitted just right and talked at length about how each one worked, outlining the steps Alice and Alex each needed to take to get the most out of them. For Alice, he was careful to make sure she understood how to manage her fracture with the new prosthetic. She listened, wide-eyed and silent, taking in every word that he said.

For Alex, the approach was different. Once his new limb was fitted and all the final adjustments had been made to allow for his particular walking gait, Dr. Mario invited him to try it out by walking around the room.

He watched as Alex took his first steps. He was tentative at first, but soon was more confident, pushing up and away with each stride like he was in a shoe store and trying on a new pair of sneakers.

"Hey," Dr. Mario said after Alex had completed his second lap of the room and was at the end of a long, empty corridor. "You know, everybody runs on their first day."

Alex turned and looked at him, not quite sure if he'd heard correctly.

"You should run," Dr. Mario repeated. "Everybody does it."

Alex stood still. "I'm going to run," he said, the words unfamiliar in his mouth. "I'm going to run. But I'm nervous."

"Why?"

"I'm afraid of falling."

"You can do it."

For a moment the room was perfectly still. Alice was sitting quietly at the far side of the room, watching the team make adjustments to her new prosthetic, while everybody on the other side had their eyes locked on Alex.

"But if I fall," he said to nobody in particular, "I'll get up again."

Then he put his head down, leaned forward, and ran.

The whole center was filled with the noise of his sneakers squeaking on the floor and the soft thud of his footsteps.

"I'm going to go again." With that—wearing a huge grin on his face—Alex pushed off the wall, turned around, and ran again. This time he ran even harder, flying down the corridor like it was a one-hundred-meter track and he was racing against some long-standing rival. He slammed into the wall at the end and paused. Eyes lost in the middle distance. Deep breaths as he drank in the air.

"Alex. Alex?" It was one of the guys videoing. "When was the last time you ran?"

The tears came immediately—a full-on sprint from a standing start. "Five years," he said between sobs. "Not since the accident. And I loved running. I loved it so much. I thought I'd never run again."

See Alex run, scan QR Code

* * *

We'd just finished our session at the conference when my phone lit up with a call from Alex. He and Alice crowded the screen.

"You should have seen it," Alice said, her face the brightest, most joy-filled I'd seen at any point on the ride. "It was so incredible. He never thought he'd run again, but he just ran, Evan. He ran!"

There's no way that I could imagine what it must have been like for Alex. I've tried many times to put myself in his position, but I can't imagine what it must be like to be told I would never run again. I've had my struggles in life just like anyone else has, but ever since I was a kid, God has given me a family, food, shoes, clothes, and everything I've needed. I've never really known what it's like to lose something so fundamental and so precious as the freedom of being able to run. I've never known that loss, but I could feel Alex's joy.

At that point I lost it. I was a blubbering mess and was hardly able to take in the rest of the conversation as they both showed off their brand-new limbs.

When the call was over I grabbed Paul and hugged him tight.

"This is all because of you, Paul. It's all because you had this crazy idea to cross North America and then came to visit me at my house. You had the vision and the guts to do it in the first place, and you helped me have the faith to do it myself."

Paul was crying just as hard as I was. "It's all because of Jesus," he choked out.

Adrian was there too, his face just as streaked with tears as mine and Paul's. He and I hugged, and when we could finally talk I told him how grateful I was for everything he'd done, how he'd worked so hard throughout even though I'd been such a jerk on that first day.

"None of that matters," he said. "God was at work all along."

"You know," said Paul. "I'd go another thousand miles to see Jesus move in someone's life like this again."

* * *

The next morning, I took Alice and Alex out shoe shopping. We found the biggest store we could in Córdoba and stood in front of the walls of sneakers, the air sweet with that fresh shoe smell.

"What kind of shoes do you guys like?" I asked.

They both looked confused and hesitant.

"I've never done this before," said Alice.

"Me neither."

I didn't understand. "What about before the accident? You bought shoes then, right?"

"Not from a store," said Alice. "We'd just buy them from whoever's selling them on the street."

Alex's eyes wandered. "And there's never anything like this selection."

It was hard for me to imagine what it had been like for Alex to not be able to run, but going sneaker shopping for the first time? That was something I could easily relate to. I always loved that time when my shoes would crack apart or they developed those little mounds where my toes were pushing against the end. I loved going to the mall, loved standing in front of them all and choosing. It always felt like the first time.

"Well," I said, "this is going to be fun."

We spent over an hour in the store, browsing through the different brands and styles. The boxes piled up around us as Alice and Alex tried shoes on, and by the time we were done, they both walked out with a solid pair of Nikes on their feet and a big smile on their faces. It sounds strange, and maybe even a little shallow, to say that shopping for a pair of quality sneakers gave their dignity and self-confidence a boost, but it did. Living in poverty had led Alice and Alex to believe that they'd never be able to shop in stores like that, and that in some way they didn't deserve to. It's a messed-up world we live in, but God is a good Father who gives good gifts. Sometimes those gifts are big, sometimes small, but they all share the same purpose of drawing our hearts and our eyes back to Him.

* * *

Ciclo Vida got me thinking about a lot of things, from what it takes to be a good leader and how easy it is to be a bad one, to what it means to witness a genuine, God-ordained miracle. But on that Saturday—from the time we walked out of the shoe store to the moment later that evening when we worshiped with thousands of others and unleashed our joy and gratitude to God—I was thinking about identity.

When I was twenty a pastor sat me down and told me that he had something he wanted to share. I was hungry for direction and affirmation and happy to hear from anyone who might have a word from God for me.

My father's affair when I was a little kid hadn't been the only complication in my childhood. Dad had been excommunicated from the church that he had started, had gotten remarried, and in one of those strange plot twists that seem better suited to TV than real life, my stepmom ended up having an affair as well. My dad had married again after that, but my life continued to be turbulent. Home was chaotic at best.

My uncle had taken over the church that my dad

had started. He made a thing of telling people that he wasn't anything like his brother and that he was not going to make the same mistakes. We all believed it was a time of redemption, but it eventually turned to tragedy. He fell into unfaithfulness as well.

Everybody in the area knew my family's checkered history, and for some, I guess we were a cautionary tale. For me, it was complicated, and I was still trying to figure it all out when I was twenty.

So when the pastor asked to talk to me, I gladly took a seat beside him and told him I was all ears.

"I'm sorry that your father was an adulterer," he began. "So was your uncle." His message was clear: These things run in the family, so I'd better be extra careful.

I waited for him to finish. I wanted him to say, "But there's hope for you, Evan. It doesn't have to be that way." But he didn't. He just left me there, weighed down by the inevitability of it all.

I had spent more than a decade feeling confused about these aspects of my life, but I wasn't in any doubt about what I'd just heard. I knew it was wrong. I didn't know why and I didn't know what to say in response, but I knew it was wrong. How could it be that I was chained up and bound to make the same mistakes as my father or my uncle? Everything I'd ever learned about God told me otherwise. He's the loving God of second chances and hope restored, not a bully who condemns us and turns His back.

It wasn't until I was in seminary, a couple of years after that conversation with the pastor, that I finally had something more than a gut response to knock back his argument.

We were looking at two passages where Jesus healed people: the paralytic man who had been lowered through the roof and the woman who was continually bleeding.

To the paralytic man Jesus said: "Son, your sins are forgiven" (Mark 2:5).

And to the woman He said: "Daughter, your faith has made you well; go in peace, and be healed of your disease" (Mark 5:34).

Son… Daughter…

These are the only times when Jesus addresses anyone this way. Yes, it's about forgiveness of sins and miraculous physical healing, but those two words— “son… daughter…”—stand out because what Jesus is doing is so incredibly powerful: After years of being defined by their pain and humiliation, He’s restoring their identity. He’s breaking their chains. He’s affirming them as the people they were created to be, not the pain they have endured along the way.

When I heard this in seminary, I lost it. I knew that I’d make plenty of my own mistakes, but not necessarily the same ones my father and uncle made. I knew then that I am free to have a healthy marriage, free to have a life that was full of the goodness God had ordained for me. My identity came from Him, nowhere else.

In his book *The Liberating Mission of Jesus*, the Peruvian pastor and writer Dario Lopez Rodriguez explains how Jesus operates and interacts with us. He does not keep His distance. He does not push us away. He does not act as an observer to our lives, our pain, our struggles. Instead, He draws close to us. Jesus gets down from the balcony.

He joins us in the dirt.

He walks with us.

* * *

On that Saturday night in Córdoba, Alice and Alex walked onstage with their shiny new prosthetics and their pristine sneakers. Alice told her story; Alex sang his song. They looked more alive than I'd ever seen them at any point on the ride. Something had changed within them, and I knew it was more than just the gifts they had been given. It was their identities. They'd been called *son* and *daughter* by God Himself. After all those years they'd spent worrying that they were nothing more than a burden, after that long, agonizing dark night when Alex had longed for suicide, God was rewriting the story. He was showing them that they were not a burden, that they were loved and valued and cherished by their Father in heaven. He was reminding them that He had gotten down from the balcony. And because God can't be anything other than a good and loving God, He restored that which had been cut away from them on the surgeon's table.

"We never could have expected this much," said Alex. "It's been incredible. God has shown us that He knows exactly what we need."

We sang even louder after that. Essence was dancing as wild and free as anyone I'd ever seen. Paul was on guitar, giving it everything just like he was leading the peloton up into the Andes again. When we were midway through "The Extra Mile," I heard a ripple of delight spread through the crowd and looked back to see Alex had brought his bike onstage and was riding it in circles, weaving in and out of the band.

Identity restored.

Chapter Ten

After We Fall

Back when this all began—when I first thought about taking my guitar and moving south of the border—I wanted to see miracles. I wanted to see sight restored, tumors removed, and limbs grown back. I wanted to see the dead raised back to life, just like Reinhard Bonnke had witnessed.

Seven years had passed, and I'd not seen anything like that at all. I'd seen God at work, that was for sure. But miracles? The tally was stubbornly stuck at zero.

And yet, as I stood onstage and watched the balloons fall on the thousands of people I'd never met before but with whom I was sharing this beautiful moment of unfiltered, raw worship of God, I wondered.

I looked at Alex, riding his bike around the stage, as free and euphoric as any man I'd ever seen. He could run. He could ride without pain. He was free from so much that had once chained him.

I looked at Alice, still using those crutches but with a joy and peace shining out from her that could have eclipsed the sun. She still had a ways to go, still needed to heal, but finally, seven years after it was taken from her, she had hope restored.

God hadn't just worked on a physical level for both Alice and Alex. He had addressed their emotional pain and brought them into salvation. Not one miracle but three.

I'd been looking for a miracle, and there it was. It didn't look like the ones I'd scripted, but who else but God could have woven all these people, these events, together to create such a dramatic change?

In many ways Córdoba felt like the climax of the ride. It was the point at which the purpose of *Ciclo Vida* was revealed to us all, the moment when the mist cleared and the sun shone through. Yet when we were finished in Córdoba, there were still three days of riding left before we could dip our tires into the Atlantic in Buenos Aires and call the ride good. We tackled those two hundred miles without incident, and in this final section it felt like we were covering half as much. The conditions were far from perfect, and we encountered a mixture of hailstorms and shifting winds that only once were at our backs. What made the difference was the way we approached those days. After we had seen Alice and Alex receive their new prosthetics in Córdoba, we were full of life and faith. We had fire in our bellies. *Ciclo Vida* had changed the lives of two of our friends, and now there was no limit to our optimism.

We did a concert in Rosario, then traveled south to the town of San Nicolás de los Arroyos and the home of Ulises Eyherabide, an Argentinian Christian artist and genuine legend of the Latin American music scene. He was a gracious host and had invited us to put on a beautiful *asado*—a classic Argentinian barbecue with enough meat to fuel us for a whole other *Ciclo Vida*.

Sitting around the table in Ulises's home, our bellies as full as our hearts, I looked around at the eighteen of us, grateful for what every single one had brought to the ride. We came from everywhere—not just the United States and Venezuela, but Guatemala, Colombia, El Salvador, and Costa Rica—and some of us had started out as strangers. Now we were friends. We felt like a family. We had formed deep connections with each other, learning to lean on each other when in need of strength and when to lead when others were tired. It was a beautiful thing to see. And it wasn't quite over yet.

I watched Alex lean close to Alice, say something, and stand up from the table. He led her out of the dining room, onto the patio outside.

The room hushed as others noticed the pair of them standing there. We couldn't hear what he was saying, but we could see the effect his words were having on Alice. She was staring at him like he was the only other living creature alive on the planet.

We watched as he took a step back from her. Saw her hands go to her face as Alex knelt down on one knee—a move that his old prosthetic would never have allowed him to pull off so easily. His hand went into his pocket and came out with a ring. For the first time since they'd left the room, Alice's eyes were torn from Alex's face. She stared at the ring, tears on her cheeks. Then she looked back at Alex and mouthed the word *sí*.

I had no idea that Alex was going to propose. I found out later that he'd only just bought the ring when we were in Córdoba. But it made perfect sense, and I was so happy for them. To me, it said so much about how the ride had impacted them. Instead of feeling like they were trapped, they now saw a future for themselves. Instead of seeing God as a remote, distant deity, they now saw Him as a truly loving Father before whom they wanted to stand and make their vows.

That was the moment when I realized something else about the ride. I finally saw the extent to which love was at the very heart of *Ciclo Vida*. I'd started out thinking that the aim of the ride was to raise money and give it away in the hope of changing a few lives. Now I saw that *Ciclo Vida* was about more than that. The ride had brought all of us closer together, not just Alice and Alex. It showed us that we can do so much more when we are connected to and supported by others—that when we go The Extra Mile in the name of our faith, we likely won't travel alone. God will bring others across our path, some so that we can encourage them, some to be an encouragement to us.

We shouldn't be surprised by this. After all, it's how Jesus operated, pulling together a band of disciples, apostles, and other followers. And when it came time for fieldwork, He didn't send them out solo either, but in pairs. We were created to be in communion, with God and with each other. We were built to partner with others—even the ones who let us down, hurt us, or get unreasonable and hangry and shout at us outside of gas stations. We were made for this, mess and all.

In Alice and Alex, I saw a reflection of the kind of wild, dramatic, extraordinary, selfless, generous, supportive love that bears all the hallmarks of God's own love for us. As they came back into the house and we cheered and yelled and spent the next hours singing and laughing and celebrating with them, the sense that God was smiling on us all was almost tangible. In a strange way, just like Alice and Alex each had new limbs at the end of the ride, each of us had grown a little more whole, been restored a little more to the fullness of life for which we were created.

* * *

The last day of cycling took us right into the heart of Buenos Aires. There was some kind of strike going on that day, which meant that there were no 18-wheelers on the road. It felt strange not to be sharing the highway with those big beasts, but as we rode closer to the city, the roads grew bigger and the traffic became more congested and manic. Eventually, we were riding along a five-lane freeway with concrete dividers, overpasses, off-ramps, and cars passing within two feet of us while they sped along at sixty miles per hour. It was a white-knuckle ride for several miles, and we were slower than we'd planned. Eventually, our route took us off the freeway and onto some side roads for the final two miles. We were two hours later than we had planned, but it didn't matter so much. After 1,200 miles over seventeen days, we were just about done.

Then Essence got a flat.

We were a mile away from our finish line—where a small crowd of people were waiting to celebrate with us—but we ground to a complete halt. We hadn't had a single flat in three weeks of riding, not since that first morning when we couldn't go fifteen minutes without needing to stop and change a tire. But here we were, stuck in a side street, waiting.

I wish I could say that I sat there, full of peace and grace, not allowing the delay to get to me in any way. That would be a lie. Instead, for just a few moments, I found it excruciating. Even though I know it's vital not to leave anyone behind, even at the end of the challenge, I was desperate to finish, to complete the task that we had officially set out to achieve. I wanted to finish strong, to cross the line and see the people who had come to help us celebrate.

In other words, I was feeling the urge to be an artist, not a soldier.

Ciclo Vida wasn't ever about impressing people with our riding. I knew that deep down, but at that moment when we stopped for Essence to change her tire, with the finish line so close yet our progress at a halt, I forgot it for just a little while. Just long enough to be reminded of my place in this whole God-scripted adventure.

It strikes me that God teaches us a lot of stuff when we're behaving like toddlers. We might be adults, but when we're too tired, too sad, too hungry, or too worried to be able to talk ourselves down, that's when we need a loving parent to come and scoop us up in their big arms. And often, just as He's providing the rest, the comfort, the fuel, or the calm that we need, God shines a light on the places we need Him the most.

Soon we were on the way again. It seemed like it only took us a few seconds to reach our finish line in downtown Buenos Aires, and a few more for the tears to start to flow. After we had celebrated with the fifty or sixty people who had come to see us, we got back on our bikes and cycled the final five miles of the ride out to the coast, so we could end the ride as we began, with our tires dipped in the ocean.

We rode in silence.

It felt right to be ending this way, and not just for the symmetry of starting in the Pacific and ending in the Atlantic. It felt right to end it quietly, with just the riders and the video guys. It felt right to go the extra few miles, and it felt right to take time and reflect. Soldiers, not artists.

* * *

There were two more concerts to do in Buenos Aires. They were every bit as profound and powerful as the others. We sang free, danced wild, and knew that there was nothing left to do but thank God for the opportunity to say yes to this whole adventure. After the final concert, as we sat around a TV in a crowded hotel room and watched as the video guys showed us some of their favorite footage, it started to get emotional.

For some of the band, this was the first time they had been away from their family for so long. After five weeks of being on the road, they were ready to go home. They had used up all their strength and needed a serious recharge.

For Alice and Alex, the idea of going home stirred different tears.

"We don't want to go back to Venezuela," Alex said when almost everyone else had crashed out.

I wasn't surprised, but I had that same sense of responsibility and duty that I'd experienced when Alice had first talked about staying on day one of the ride. I knew them better now, loved them more deeply, and was more committed to helping them than ever before. I was also aware how important it was to follow through with anything I promised. I didn't want to be another hard lesson that God taught them through.

"Okay," I said. "I'll push your return flights back as far as I can. If you want to go home sooner, we can change them back. Where are you going to go? Chile?"

"Dr. Mario said that if we lived in Córdoba, he would connect us with other people and make sure that our prosthetics are working fine."

It was a kind and generous offer that was too good to refuse, but I wondered whether they really knew what it would be like to start a new life in Córdoba, or anywhere in Argentina or Chile. Ever since we'd left Rosario, Alice had been asking me when and where the next *Ciclo Vida* was going to take place. For the last five weeks, they'd been surrounded by friends, and the team had taken care of everything—food, accommodations, entertainment, and all the rest. It had been hard work, there was no doubt about it, but it wasn't real life. I wondered whether they were hanging their hopes on a version of life that simply wasn't possible. Were they setting themselves up for disappointment?

I was trying to figure out how to say all of this when Alice interrupted my thoughts.

"It won't be easy, we know that, Evan. That's why my motto is, *if the pros fall, we'll probably fall as well.*"

"And if we do fall," added Alex, "we'll get up and continue. What else can we do?"

* * *

I said goodbye to everyone over the course of the next day. The band flew back to Colombia, Pablo to Miami, Paul to LA, and Essence to Orange County, where she would once again be reunited with Nathan and begin married life together. Alice and Alex were heading to Córdoba and were excited about their new life ahead of them.

I stayed back for one more day. After five weeks living and working with so many people, I was looking forward to some quiet downtime. I had some thinking to do and some plans to make.

I found myself sitting in a café in Buenos Aires, thinking back over the ride. It had been hands down my favorite thing that I'd ever done in my life. I'd seen the vastness of creation and realized how small I was within it. I'd been able to tangibly, practically help people in ways that, as an artist, I rarely felt like I was able to do.

I'd started it wanting to do something that would give to others. Along the way I discovered that God was also pouring healing and goodness into my own life as well. He'd shown me that I don't need to ever doubt what He can do. I don't need to question His provision, and I don't need to second-guess His moves. All I need to do is keep going along the path He's set for me, and trust Him through every trial and triumph, every obstacle and opportunity that comes my way.

I felt different. I didn't know for sure, but I had a hunch that the ride had cured me of the sense of boredom and purposelessness that had troubled me since the massive concert in Bogotá. And while I didn't know whether *Ciclo Vida* would ever happen again, I shared Alice's hunger for whatever God was inviting me to jump into next.

Isn't that the truth? When we say yes to God, we don't know the twists and turns in the adventure ahead. Maybe it's better that way. Maybe that's how God keeps us alert and open to Him. What I do know is that of all the wisdom I've picked up along the way, some of my favorite is this, right here:

> *Life isn't easy. That's a fact*
> *If the pros fall, we'll fall as well.*
> *When we do fall, we'll get right up*
> *and keep fighting.*
> *What else can we do?*

What Next?

(A Conclusion)

WITHIN THREE DAYS of arriving back to my apartment in Medellín, I realized I didn't need to be there anymore. It was time to move on. Not just from the apartment, the city, and the friends I had made there that year. It was time to move on from Colombia, to go back to the States, if only for a while. Having felt so alive on the ride, having rediscovered in the mountains and flat lands of Chile and Argentina the sense of purpose and calling that had been missing from my life, there was a part of me that was surprised to feel that this season in Latin America was coming to an end. But it was, and I knew that God was opening a new door for me, one in which I would continue to go deeper in my faith and strengthen my knowledge of Him. I was going back to seminary, moving to Lakeland, Florida, to complete the degree I had started years earlier but never finished. I'd fallen in love with the people of Latin America and completing seminary would allow me to return to them better equipped.

I was excited and a little nervous, just like Alice and Alex in Córdoba. But just like them, I was going into this new journey with the truths learned on *Ciclo Vida* still ringing loud within my heart.

The truth that God has called us to go beyond the status quo. We were made with a purpose: to bring the hope of Jesus to people around us, and to express His love in tangible, real ways. We were made to go The Extra Mile.

The truth that when we say yes to God and step out of our comfort zone and go beyond society's expectations of us, we begin to truly live.

The truth that God's expectations and plans for our lives are often very different from our own.

The truth that when we step onto the battlefield

like David facing Goliath, or out of the boat like Peter, God shows up. All we have to do is keep our eyes fixed on Jesus.

The truth that God is not confined to my imagination. The ways that God answers prayers and performed miracles are not constrained by our expectation.

* * *

Alice and Alex are still in Córdoba. Dr. Mario has been true to his word and helped them. And while life has not always been easy for them in Argentina, their eyes are still fixed on God.

Paul is now a creative pastor at a church in Austin, Texas.

Essence and Nathan are enjoying life in Southern California.

Adrian is married and opened his own publicity agency.

My sister, Lindy, is working full time in the ICU.

And me? After I finished my year of seminary

I was excited about going back and touring Latin America. Then COVID-19 happened, and all those plans were put on hold. I spent more time songwriting and found there was a new well to tap into. Out of the blue some of the songs did really well, which made me happy—but not as happy as finding out that God had another surprise in store for me. Her name is Rachel, and we married in 2021.

Recently I was reading *The Spirit of the Disciplines* by Dallas Willard, and I found something that made so much sense to me. It's in a passage that refers to Jesus' comment in Matthew 11:30, where He said, "My yoke is easy, and my burden is light." Dallas Willard points out that Jesus was only able to say it because He had developed the spiritual muscles to cope. He didn't jump into ministry at age thirty having spent His first three decades ignoring God. He prepared, and that hard work allowed Him to go The Extra Mile.

I'm so grateful for all those early mornings when Dad would wake us up to study the Bible. They were the foundations of my faith, the early years of training that started my spiritual muscles working. They were the days of small beginnings.

Today, we live with the constant bombardment of content from people who want to impress, amuse, or inspire us. It can be tempting to focus so much on the finished product—that perfect moment of skill from Kobe or Messi—that we forget about all the years of work and effort that went in to reach it. We can become so fixated on astonishing output that we forget that it is only possible because of diligent, dedicated, hard work. Our eyes are drawn to the trophies more than the journey to reach them.

Going The Extra Mile in our faith means starting small and letting God build those spiritual muscles over years and years.

So, please, don't put this book down and try to start planning your own version of a coast-to-coast cycle ride. Don't end this book with dreams of what you might accomplish in your own strength. Put it down and find your equivalent of a 5:30 a.m. Bible study. Close the cover and go out and find the people whose influence on your life will help to shape and strengthen your character. Finish this book and set your sights on drawing ever closer to God. Orient your life around loving people the way Jesus loved them. Set goals that propel you closer to the people who need God's love the most.

Live a life that is rich in purpose.

Love people.

Serve them.

Go The Extra Mile.

Acknowledgments

THIS ADVENTURE was inspired by Paul Joung. Thank you for challenging me and letting me pretend I can keep up with you in sports.

Thank you, Essence and Nathan Jasperse, for coming the week after your wedding.

Pablo Espindola for sharing the gospel every night and encouraging me when I didn't think I could go on.

Adrian Villalobos, for moving to Medellín with me, organizing everything, and still being my friend after all the ups and downs I've put you through.

Alice and Alex, we love you guys and believe that God has great things in store for you. We love you and your precious baby!

Deborah, Kathryn, Bito, David, José, Daniel, Sebas, Javier, Jean Paul, we couldn't have done this without you.

Thank you to every pastor and church from Viña del Mar all the way to Buenos Aires. I pray for blessings on you and your congregation, and we hope to return and worship together again soon!

Thank you, Señora Villa, for inspiring a love for Spanish.

Thank you, Craig Borlase, for bringing this story to life.

And thank you, K-LOVE BOOKS, for bringing it to the world!

About the Author

Evan Craft has earned recognition for seamlessly bridging the gap between English- and Spanish-speaking audiences. Following the success of his latest releases—*Más Rico Del Mundo*, his sixth full-length Spanish album, and *Chances*, his newest English project—Craft continues to solidify his place in the global music landscape. His 2012 breakthrough album, *Yo Soy Segundo*, became a Billboard-charting Latin sensation, establishing him as a powerful voice in both languages.

With nearly 2 billion global streams to his name, Craft's music resonates deeply within the Latino community and beyond. Beyond his music, he's committed to making a real-world impact. Through events like Mi Casa LA and Good Neighbor Nights, he has raised $500,000 for homeless initiatives in Los Angeles, embodying the authenticity and heart that his fans admire.

Evan is married to Rachel, and they have two daughters. Together, they are passionate about challenging others to live a life of faith and purpose, working to encourage others to follow Jesus.

STAY UP TO DATE ON MUSIC, TOUR, AND LATEST NEWS AT
WWW.EVANCRAFTMUSIC.COM